THINKING FOR CLINICIANS

THINKING FOR CLINICIANS

Philosophical Resources for Contemporary
Psychoanalysis and the
Humanistic Psychotherapies

Donna M. Orange

Routledge
Taylor & Francis Group
New York   London

Routledge
Taylor & Francis Group
270 Madison Avenue
New York, NY 10016

Routledge
Taylor & Francis Group
27 Church Road
Hove, East Sussex BN3 2FA

© 2010 by Taylor and Francis Group, LLC
Routledge is an imprint of Taylor & Francis Group, an Informa business

Printed in the United States of America on acid-free paper
10 9 8 7 6 5 4 3 2 1

International Standard Book Number: 978-0-88163-492-1 (Hardback) 978-0-88163-493-8 (Paperback)

Library of Congress Cataloging-in-Publication Data

Orange, Donna M.
    Thinking for clinicians : philosophical resources for contemporary
psychoanalysis and the humanistic psychotherapies / Donna M. Orange.
        p. cm.
    Includes bibliographical references and index.
    ISBN 978-0-88163-492-1 (hardcover) -- ISBN 978-0-88163-493-8 (pbk.)
    1. Psychoanalysis--Philosophy. 2. Humanistic psychotherapy--Philosophy. I.
Title.

    RC506.O695 2009
    616.89'17--dc22   2009004258

Visit the Taylor & Francis Web site at
http://www.taylorandfrancis.com

and the Routledge Web site at
http://www.routledgementalhealth.com

For Don,

and in memory of Henny

CONTENTS

Acknowledgments   ix

Chapter 1   Introduction
            Psychotherapy in a Socratic Spirit   1

Chapter 2   Martin Buber
            The Dialogic We   15

Chapter 3   Ludwig Wittgenstein
            Nothing Is Hidden   35

Chapter 4   Maurice Merleau-Ponty
            Embodied Intersubjectivity   55

Chapter 5   Emmanuel Levinas
            Trauma and the Face of the Other   77

Chapter 6   Hans-Georg Gadamer
            Undergoing the Situation With the Other   99

Afterword   119
Glossary   121
References   127
Index   139

ACKNOWLEDGMENTS

Acknowledgments is a feeble word for the gratitude I owe to the people, dead and alive, who have helped me to write this book. First are my philosophical mentors: Frances Madden, Andrew Bjelland, Thomas Royce, Max Fisch, Quentin Lauer, Manfred Frank, and most recently, Simon Critchley. In psychoanalysis, my colleagues at IPSS (Institute for the Psychoanalytic Study of Subjectivity, New York), and ISIPSé (Istituto di Specializzazione in Psicologia Psicoanalitica del Sé e Psicoanalisi Relazionale, Roma) have been a tremendous support. My two collaborators on previous books, George Atwood and Robert Stolorow, whom I affectionately call "the boys," supported me and believed in me long before I ever thought of writing books. My classes, workshops, and study groups in Rome, New York, and elsewhere have impelled me to write this book. The welcome I have felt in these places, and recently as well among gestalt therapy colleagues, has made me feel that I am connecting all of you with my old best friends, these philosophers.

For both inspiration and reading of drafts, I thank George Atwood, Doris Brothers, Elizabeth Corpt, Roger Frie, Jackie Gotthold, Michael Reison, Robert Stolorow, and Jonathan Watkins. Both Lynne Jacobs and Donald Braue have read the entire manuscript at least once each. Of course, these friends are not responsible for my opinions and mistakes, but still, I have no words to express what this group of colleagues has meant to me or how much they have improved this book. "You lift me up . . ."

Kristopher Spring and Kate Hawes of Routledge (Taylor & Francis) have made me feel this book was wanted and have patiently waited for it and brought it into the world. My production editor, Robert Sims, gives new meaning to Howard Bacal's expression "optimal responsiveness."

Finally, words like *spouse, partner, best friend*, even *rock of Gibraltar*, do not begin to capture what Don has been and done for me along the way. There is an old saying that those who love sausages and philosophies should never watch them being made. He makes me feel it is a privilege and a participation.

1

INTRODUCTION

Psychotherapy in a Socratic Spirit

The unexamined life is not worth living.

—Socrates

Contemporary clinicians face continual challenges: our everyday struggles to understand and heal by way of the "talking cure"; the conflicts
between old and new ideas in psychoanalytic theory and practice; the
challenge of developmental thinking; the need to recognize our work
as situated historically, culturally, and politically; the pervasiveness of
cognitive neuroscience, of "evidence-based" treatments like cognitive-
behavioral approaches, biological/pharmacological reductionism, and
many more. To meet these challenges, training in psychoanalysis and
in other humanistic forms of psychotherapy usually provides a strong
acquaintance with the major thinkers in each tradition, along with
considerable orientation to the emotional and relational processes and
challenges involved. Often, however, good and gifted clinicians, even
those with long experience, seem to feel inadequate as readers of their
own literatures.

This book aims to provide working clinicians with tools and context
for thinking about psychotherapeutic work and theories. It assumes
that some background in the history of Western philosophy—in which
our sources such as Freud, Fairbairn, Kohut, Loewald, the Gestalt psychologists, Mitchell, and Stolorow have been well grounded—would
help us to understand them. In addition, some acquaintance with 20th-
century philosophers would be helpful to those wanting to read with

more understanding and critical acumen. North American clinicians who come to me for supervision and for study groups often describe themselves as "intimidated by theory" and ashamed of their anxiety about conceptual work, but interested and willing to learn to read it capably. By introducing philosophers into the conversation, this book aims to induce both curiosity and a sense of feeling more at home and competent in the world of ideas.

Socrates remains the dominant ideal for Western philosophy. Simple-living, ever-questioning, relentlessly seeking the good human life, he exasperated the Athenians. Having questioned a man reputed to be wise, he thought to himself, "I am wiser than this man; it is likely that neither of us knows anything worthwhile, but he thinks he knows something when he does not, whereas when I do not know, neither do I think I know; so I am likely to be wiser than he to this small extent, that I do not think I know what I do not know" (Plato, trans. 1997, p. 21).* He saw the Athenians' preference for persuasion over thinking as endangering their youth, yet they accused *him* of "corrupting the youth." Finding that they could not silence him, the Athenians offered him the choice of silence or death. He responded: "You are wrong, sir, if you think that a man who is any good at all should take into account the risk of life or death; he should look to this only in his actions, whether what he does is right or wrong, whether he is acting like a good or bad man" (p. 26).†

This book addresses clinicians whose personal and professional ideals resemble those of Socrates. From many traditions—especially psychoanalytic and humanistic—such psychotherapists long to understand, but know how little we know. We are always questioning our assumptions, our reactions, and the inevitable limitations of our points of view. Our field is human emotional life—in particular, the lives of those suffering others (the word *patient* coming from the Latin *patior*, meaning to suffer) who come to us full of hope and dread (Mitchell, 1993): hope that a human connection may save them, and dread that it may fail them once more. In short, here is the thesis of this book: Thoughtful psychoanalysts and other humanistic clinicians are practicing philosophers. Doing philosophy every day, we always need to think more about what we are unconsciously doing. Engaging in dialogue with great philosophers can help us to keep thinking and questioning. If we clinicians do not engage, we remain captives in an unexamined life, in the grip of philosophical assumptions we notice neither in our theory nor in our practice.

---

* Apology 21d, in the standard way of citing Plato's works.
† Apology, 28b-c.

From the time of Freud, psychoanalysts and other clinicians have tried to theorize the emotional life, its development and failure. For Freud, the life of sexual and aggressive instincts, primarily unconscious, played out in disguises, a life full of conflict with itself and with external reality. For Kleinians, fundamental and original aggression was emotional bedrock, explaining everything. For the British middle group (especially Winnicott), as well as for Kohutian self psychology, self-development within the family succeeded or failed. For relational psychoanalysis,* including intersubjective systems theory, concepts like relational matrix, intersubjective field, and attachment systems have gained currency. All these theories remain dependent on their philosophical underpinnings.

As a young man, Freud aspired to be a philosopher (Herzog, 1988). He took five courses from proto-phenomenologist Franz Brentano and translated a volume of John Stuart Mill's work, including *The Subjection of Women* (Mill & Freud, 1880), into German. Unfortunately, perhaps due to his passion to be thought original, he disavowed having read Nietzsche and Schopenhauer—both of whose work prefigured his own concept of the unconscious—and then contemptuously claimed that philosophers had nothing to contribute to his thinking.

So psychoanalysis, heir both to Freud's incapacity to engage differences of opinion and to its own dogmatisms, has frequently failed clinicians and has often abandoned the Socratic project. Psychoanalysis, for the most part, treated clinical work as independent of its philosophical context and thus protected its theories from both in-house and external criticism. Thus, a plurality of humanistic psychotherapies arose independently and now constitutes a community that only partly overlaps in spirit and theory with psychoanalysis, even in its contemporary and more relational versions. Groups like the relational gestalt therapists (e.g., Lynne Jacobs and Frank-M. Staemmler), the existential-humanist children of Abraham Maslow, Rollo May, Carl Rogers, Viktor Frankl, and Eugene Gendlin (perhaps grandchildren of Ludwig Binswanger and Martin Buber), as well as others whom I know less well, are among the clinicians who attempt to live the Socratic ideal.

WHY THINKING MATTERS

Assuming no sharp distinction between feeling and thinking, I see at least five reasons for clinicians to care about thinking. These include (a) undoing

---

* Relational psychoanalysis is both an inclusive designation ("relational") and a specific school ("Relational"); see glossary.

shame (Orange, 2008c), (b) resisting cults, (c) helping us to notice, (d) keeping us clinically creative, and (e) loosening the grip of automaticity.

First, student-colleagues often say to me, "I'm not a theorist or philosopher; I'm just a clinician, and this is all that interests me." This sounds like a reasonable acceptance of one's personal gifts and limitations, but I am not so sure. Many, when I inquire further, explain that they are ashamed of their fear of theory and philosophy, of concepts and of logic. Studying these areas—usually neglected in American university education—threatens to expose, to oneself and others, a sense of profound personal and professional inadequacy. It seems better to dismiss philosophy as unimportant than to feel such a shameful lack. For some, the teacher who challenges such students to read philosophy deserves the fate of Socrates.

This book, nevertheless, addresses these colleagues, among others. It invites thinking as active engagement in organizing our everyday clinical experience, of "the given," as philosophers say. Each chapter invites us to meet the philosopher as a human being in the context of his own life and historical circumstances, and so to understand his thinking. Next, each chapter addresses some difficulties the philosopher's style— not to mention the problems of reading translations from French or German—may create for readers. The idea here is to make reading easier and to mitigate the strangeness. Each chapter next focuses on one or more central ideas and shows how a clinician who has absorbed such ideas might work differently. Above all, each chapter attempts to intrigue the reader enough that she or he might want to try reading the philosophers in the primary sources. In case a reader takes a special interest in one philosopher, a few accessible "further reading" suggestions follow each chapter, and the reference list provides many more sources. Along the way, a concise glossary may help readers to avoid getting stuck. All these elements attempt to sneak around the fear of feeling inadequate and ashamed.

Second, we need to think and question every time we become enamored with a single thinker or school of thought. Every psychoanalytic or psychotherapeutic hero or heroine can become our guru, even our cult leader. Seduced by such authorities—either world class or local— we can abandon our human responsibility to think and question. Instead, we are tempted to interpret the world, our clinical experience, and worst of all, our patients through the voice of the cult leader. We may join groups (including training institutes) that exclude, dominate, and disallow dissenting voices. I believe that reading philosophy is the best antidote for this trouble that has beset our field from the time of Freud. As philosophy students, we become "perpetual beginners" like

Edmund Husserl, father of the phenomenological movement (Moran, 2000, p. 62). As beginners, we remain less likely to think we already know or to place too much faith in the "knowing" of others, even those others whom our own training prepares us to treat with too much reverence. If philosophers themselves become cult leaders or gurus, they are no longer really philosophers for those who follow.

Third, reading philosophy teaches us to read and listen differently and to notice what we might miss if we read only the theoretical formulations of our own tradition. Above all, we may notice the anomalies in our own clinical experience. Why does saying and doing what I have been taught seem not to work in this situation? The great innovators in psychoanalysis and in the humanistic psychotherapies have been people who could notice, and even foreground, what their own theory had made invisible or had relegated to the background because it did not fit the theory. They noticed patients who had not been helped by their theory, they noticed new developmental studies, and they noticed intellectual developments like relativity and quantum physics, chaos and complexity theories. They found themselves questioned not only by their colleagues but by what they allowed themselves to notice.

Fourth, thinking supports creativity. This idea may seem counterintuitive to some. Granted, obsessive overthinking can paralyze our creative capacities. But underthinking, just going along with what we have always thought or with what authorities teach, also stifles us. When we begin to read philosophy, once we get past the initial language barriers, we not only notice but start to see differently, as if from new perspectives that stretch our own. Our attempts to make sense of divergent perspectives on human experience, especially when pursued within conversation, can evoke from us thoughts and expressions we did not have before. Some historians (Melchert, 2002) have seen philosophy as a "great conversation." Even we who feel incapable of such a grand conversation can involve ourselves through reading and conversation with thinkers whose own questioning participation in the "great conversation" draws us in. We can then innovatively bring the thinker's questions and insights into dialogue with our own clinical concerns and traditions.

Finally, thinking and reading philosophy can loosen the grip of automaticity on our clinical lives. It can teach us to question our presuppositions, "organizing principles" (Stolorow, Atwood, & Brandchaft, 1987), or emotional convictions (Orange, 1995) that keep such a grip on us. Held by these automaticities, we react instead of responding thoughtfully. Philosophy, on the contrary, unsettles us. The skepticism about received ideas, inherent in most philosophy—Western or otherwise— can make us theoretical and clinical fallibilists. Fallibilism (Orange,

1995) characterizes both the thought and practice of a contextualist. It means that we recognize that our present understanding of anything or anyone is only a perspective within a horizon inevitably limited by the historicity of our own organized and organizing experience (Orange, 2009b). In practice, a contextualist holds lightly not only theory but any particular view of meaning in the patient's experience or in the cocreated experience in the intersubjective field of treatment. This fallibilistic attitude keeps us flexible and open to multiple, emerging, and expanding horizons of meaning. It also ensures that our theoretical ideas can continue to evolve toward an ever-richer and more encompassing viewpoint.

THE QUESTION OF HUMANISM

The title of this book addresses "contemporary psychoanalysis and the humanistic psychotherapies" and needs three clarifications. First, to prevent misunderstanding, let me say that I see most contemporary, postclassical psychoanalysts as humanists, but I leave it to them to decide if they want this designation or not. As for the philosophers, I will say a few words in each chapter about each one's version of humanism.

Second, among other psychotherapists, I see a strong divide between therapists inspired by the kind of humanism shared by the philosophers this book engages and those inspired more by the tradition of the natural sciences—Dilthey's *Naturwissenschaften* (Dilthey, 1883/1988). Among these latter are found cognitive behaviorists, neuropsychoanalysts, and practitioners of other technique-oriented therapies like EMDR (eye-movement desensitization and reprocessing). Although many of these therapists would claim—and rightly—a humanistic motivation for their work (Siegel, 1999), the methods and theories themselves may contravene a humanist's view of personal experience and can wreak havoc when practiced apart from the solidity of dialogic therapies attentive to the ongoing quality of human ties. This book's readers probably consider themselves humanists of some kind.

But, third, the concept of "humanism" itself has a checkered history in recent philosophy, coming under attack by Martin Heidegger, by animal rights advocates, and by theists. Most famously, Heidegger's 1947 "Letter on Humanism" (Heidegger, 1977) claimed that humanism was a form of Cartesian subjectivism—the isolated mind philosophy that takes human life out of the world and elevates it above the world, much as the medieval scholastics' "great chain of being" had done.* Anthropocentric humanism, Heidegger thought, denies that we are always already worlded, that we are simply being-in-the-world (Dasein). To differentiate his philosophy from the existentialism of Jean-Paul Sartre, Heidegger claimed that humanism overestimates autonomy and attributes human dignity to an exaggerated sense of liberty. By contrast with the whole humanistic tradition, he unforgettably began his "Letter on Humanism" by shifting his attention to language and Being:

> Thinking accomplishes the relation of Being to the essence of man. It does not make or cause the relation. Thinking brings this relation to Being solely as something handed over to it from Being. Such offering consists in the fact that in thinking Being comes to language. Language is the house of Being. In its home man dwells. Those who think and those who create with words are the guardians of this home. (p. 217)

For Heidegger, man (the human species) lives in the house of language, which is the house of Being. Not only did he oppose Sartre's view of freedom, but Heideggerian "thinking"—very different from the dialogic process this book concerns—is an abstract process by which "Being" appears in language. To him, the humanism of the Western philosophical tradition is another form of what he called "forgetfulness of Being."

In a second critique, animal rights philosophers have accused humanists of "speciesism," or discrimination that, like racism, discriminates unjustly. They think that, for humanists, moral status—being entitled to respectful treatment—depends only on sentience, the ability to feel (Regan & Singer, 1989; Singer, 1986). Humanists, they believe, are Darwinians in the sense that survival motivations justify whatever we may do to other species.

My own use of "humanist," to address these first two objections, acknowledges these objections without taking them as decisive. With Heidegger, I agree that Sartre's "humanistic" existentialism exaggerates the extent of our freedom and understates our situatedness (*Weltlichkeit*). On the other hand, I find that Heidegger's antihumanism seriously undertheorizes our relations with and responsibility for each other, as he merges the others into being. The philosophers discussed in this book who consider themselves humanists, as well as the humanistic psychotherapists, generally find a middle ground between

---

* These Christian philosophers envisioned the world on a kind of ladder, from inanimate being through plants, animals, humans, angels, and God.

Heidegger and Sartre on this point.* Similarly, both Buber and Levinas acknowledge, as do I, the important question about the moral status of animals, without coming to firm conclusions about what such moral status might imply.

Third, in earlier use, and in some circles today, "humanist" implied "atheist." With the possible exception of Merleau-Ponty, none of the five philosophers discussed in this book was an atheist, though none declared himself a theist, and each had a carefully nuanced way of expressing his sense of what transcends the obvious. We will pick up some of these nuances in later chapters, but for now, let us concentrate on what "humanist" means on the affirmative side.

"Humanist," as I use it, harks back to the Greeks as they emerged from a world in which the all-too-human gods pulled all the strings. These intriguing beings bore the responsibility for the havoc wreaked in the human world. As philosophy took form in the Hellenic and Hellenistic period, even the god or gods began to seem bound by moral questions. Is it good because the gods approve it, or do the gods approve it because it is good? asked Socrates. Such subversion established in the Western world the sense that humans, with their capacity to question, had their own dignity. The Stoics in particular established an ethics that saw the "will of God" in the dignity of the human.

The humanistic tradition in Europe includes a set of inclinations shared, as we will see, by the philosophers we study together in this book: (a) a Renaissance/Enlightenment preference for thought over superstition and authority; (b) an aversion to all forms of scientific reductionism or "it all comes down to" thinking; (c) a valuing of solidarity, dialogue, and inclusion; and (d) an ongoing interest in what constitutes the good human life.

So I speak of "humanistic psychotherapies" within this tradition that includes the ancient Greeks, Spinoza, Montaigne, the American pragmatists, the five philosophers considered here, and many others. I have always found myself drawn to psychoanalytic theories that share this spirit. Here is a recent formulation of my own view:

> What self psychology—both original and contemporary—brings to psychoanalysis and to the humanistically oriented psychotherapies, I believe, is a sense of empathy as way of being—with the other, an attitude that Kohut taught us to value in place of what

---

* For a rich discussion of the overlapping connections between the philosophies of the humanistic hermeneuts (Gadamer and Ricoeur), the antihumanism of Heidegger, and the humanistic psychotherapies of "third force" figures such as Gordon Allport, Carl Rogers, and Abraham Maslow, see Sass (1989).

he called "tool-and-method pride." To those who, even today, disparage self psychology as "making nice" and ignoring the darker sides of human nature, we proclaim with Terentius that we are human and that nothing human is alien to us. We believe that our involvement in humankind means that all human experience is in principle understandable through empathic dialogue, including its nonverbal or embodied forms. This means that although you or I may not be able to understand every patient, no patient, no psychosis, no cultural difference, no form of otherness lies outside the possibility of understanding by someone. Daily we psychotherapists are called to be the someone who makes the empathic stretch to include in our horizons of understanding that someone whom we find challenging, that is, difficult to understand. (Orange, 2009a, p. 238)

Such a humanism appears, in one form or another, in each philosopher we will study together.

CONTENTS

This book contains five chapters studying five 20th-century European philosophers for their contributions to our clinical thinking: Martin Buber, Ludwig Wittgenstein, Maurice Merleau-Ponty, Emmanuel Levinas, and Hans-Georg Gadamer. Their lifetimes overlapped: All five were alive from 1908 to 1951, and thus all lived through the horror of the years 1933 to 1945 and were variously affected. In a 1924 lecture on Aristotle, Martin Heidegger proclaimed, "The personality of a philosopher is of interest only to this extent: he was born at such and such a time, he worked, and died" (quoted in Grondin, 1999/2003, p. 8*). I do not agree—not surprisingly, as I have collaborated with theorists of the interweaving of biography and theory (Atwood & Stolorow, 1993)—and I thus provide some biographical backstory for each philosopher.

My order of treatment is somewhat arbitrary and could be otherwise. It depends mostly on the order of the philosophers' most productive periods.

Chapter 2 considers Martin Buber (1878–1965), whose *I and Thou* (Buber, 1970), originally published as *Ich und Du* in 1923, made him world famous. He understood and taught that to relate humanly is to meet the other as an intimate You (Thou). To meet the other within an I-It relation, inevitable and necessary as this may often be, reduces and objectifies the other. Buber challenges the clinician to meet the other as

---

* The irony of this statement—Heidegger's own life story has nearly eclipsed his enormous stature as a philosopher—is retrospectively thick.

another human being, as a dialogic partner, and not as an instance of any category.

Martin Buber's "I and Thou" philosophy has significantly influenced contemporary relational gestalt therapy but has been largely neglected by psychoanalysis. Engaging with his work is likely to engender a passion for dialogue, inclusiveness, and reverence for the otherness of the other. At the same time, it means an implied critique of theory and practice that is solipsistic (isolated-minded), reductionistic, elitist, and authoritarian. Buber becomes, for good or for ill, a clinician's and the therapeutic community's conscience.

In Chapter 3 we turn to Ludwig Wittgenstein (1889–1951), the Austrian and Cambridge philosopher who peaked, as athletes say, in the 1930s and 1940s. His key ideas—meaning-as-use, language-games, and family resemblances—have unfortunately suffered neglect among psychoanalytic and psychotherapeutic writers. Like our other philosophers, Wittgenstein eschewed all the reductionisms of scientific rationality and showed us instead the philosopher at the everyday dialogic work of finding meanings situated within contexts, just as a therapist and patient do together. His *Philosophical Investigations*, posthumously published, established him—with Heidegger—as one of the two most influential philosophers of the 20th century. This philosopher, who gave us language-games, family resemblances, and seeing-as, may seem an anomaly in this group. His writings often seem inaccessible to non-philosophers, but he too was deeply engaged with Gestalt psychology and with Freudian psychoanalysis. He offers us another language or frame from which to notice the philosophical assumptions that pervade our work and theory, especially those that decontextualize. He relentlessly involves us in the puzzles and traps that ignoring context creates. Clinicians who learn from Wittgenstein will learn to listen for the particular discourse that gives meaning to the word a patient or a writer may use and to understand his dictum that "the meaning is the use."

Chapter 4 introduces Maurice Merleau-Ponty (1908–1961), the French phenomenologist of the body-subject. His concepts of embodied intersubjectivity, and later of the flesh, drew him to appreciate Freud more than others did. He also, as a phenomenologist, led us beyond Freud in the directions that relational psychoanalysis and intersubjective systems theories have since gone. His most influential work, *The Phenomenology of Perception* (2002), appeared in French in 1945, and claimed that perception is embodied access to the world we inhabit and that inhabits us. His last work, interrupted by his sudden death, was attempting a further and more radical replacing of the Cartesian cogito by a subjectivity intertwined with others.

Merleau-Ponty's body-subject engaged in the world is another neglected resource for therapeutic theory and practice. His basic ideas constitute both an engagement with Freud, Marx, and Sartre, as well as an ongoing and radical challenge to them. Merleau-Ponty's version of the Heideggerian being-in-the-world is explicitly humanistic, in contrast to that of Heidegger himself who eschewed humanism in his search for Being. Merleau-Ponty concentrated on the embodied subject's perception (experience in and of the lifeworld), understood both as the always-already context and as personal and social engagement with it. His work therefore constitutes a continual challenge to any remaining individualism in our thought and practice. Heavily indebted to Gestalt psychology, he is also the philosopher who most clearly embraced a field theory of intersubjectivity.

Chapter 5 presents the disruptive Emmanuel Levinas (1906–1995). By reinstating ethics as first philosophy, his work breaks up the usual search for generalities, for subjectivity, for objectivity, for concepts that reduce the other to the same. The face of the suffering other, he proclaimed, places an infinite and unfulfillable demand on me: You shall not kill; you shall not leave me to die alone. You are responsible for me. One's own subjectivity is a secondary result, what philosophers call an epiphenomenon, of responding to the other who, in his or her destitution, always transcends me. Levinas presents, I believe, a forceful challenge to the contemporary focus on the psychoanalyst's or therapist's subjectivity. "It's not about you," he might have said—except as you respond to or neglect the other.

Finally, in Chapter 6, we meet the "grand old man" Hans-Georg Gadamer (1900–2002) whose philosophic hermeneutics has provided clinicians with a fallibilistic, dialogic, open-spirited concept and model for clinical understanding. His *Truth and Method* (1989), originally published in 1960, important as it has been for my own and others' thinking, pales by comparison with the 40 years of travel, learning languages, and endless conversation that followed (Gadamer, 2007). Endlessly seeking to learn from the other, he grew into a wise elder whose sense of potential dialogue extended far beyond his European home.

Gadamer, philosopher of understanding, had a passion for the actual practice and process of conversation. Like Buber, his dialogic spirit kept him open to the otherness of the other and engaged in conversation to the end of his very long life. Like Merleau-Ponty, his search was always for a situated understanding, his effective-historical consciousness, never once-for-all achieved. Like Wittgenstein, of whose work he spoke with great appreciation, his hermeneutical philosophy (in Wittgenstein, "grammatical") became an approach to understanding everything. This chapter, more than the others, will engage the postmodern denial of the possibility of understanding and dialogue and thus give the reader access to much current theoretical psychoanalytic literature. At the same time, it will argue that dialogic philosophy is a better resource than "postmodernism" for our clinical practice.

These philosophers have been my teachers, whom I wish I had known personally. Each has a face that I remember as I read and work (my readers may want to try a Web search for their photographs). In my Roman Catholic background, each person was supposed to have a patron saint, a teacher, companion, and protector. Sanctity aside, these philosophers remain my teachers, my intellectual companions during 20 years of psychoanalytic work, and my protectors from the sirens of dogmatism and cocksureness. Their work challenges me when I am tempted to read uncritically, and inspires me when my work seems hopeless. They help me to understand why I believe when I do and why I doubt when I do. They relentlessly question my thinking and my clinical practice and are thus the best of friends and mentors, as I hope one or more of them may become for the readers of this book.

QUESTIONS OF INCLUSION

My choices in this book bring up three obvious questions: (1) Why did I choose these particular philosophers? (2) Where is Heidegger? and (3) Where are the women? I will address each briefly in turn.

First, these five European philosophers have had the greatest impact on my theoretical choices and clinical thinking in the past 10 to 15 years. My earlier interests in the pragmatism of Charles Sanders Peirce (Orange, 1984) and William James have not disappeared, only receded somewhat into the background while I have studied more phenomenology and developed a serious interest in Wittgenstein. I have wanted to introduce my philosopher friends to my clinical colleagues, for all the reasons I gave above, and because each inspires me in special ways that will become evident in the chapters that follow. (Another writer, more competent than I in the history of world religions, would have included philosophers from beyond Europe).

Second, where is Martin Heidegger? A casual answer would be: He is everywhere. His influence pervades the work of Merleau-Ponty, Levinas, and Gadamer; Levinas and Gadamer were his students. Except for Wittgenstein, each philosopher engaged, minimally or constantly, with Heidegger's *Being and Time* (1962). But a more careful answer would have two parts. First is that my collaborator Robert Stolorow (2007) has written better about Heidegger and about the usefulness of his ideas for the clinical understanding of trauma than I could do, and that therefore my efforts would have been redundant. Second, I find Heidegger's actions, and especially his later silence, a tremendous betrayal of all that philosophers hold dear,* and though I recognize his greatness and his influence on my thinking, what I have to say about him appears *en passant* in the chapters that follow.

Finally, where are the women philosophers? In an era when Marcia Cavell, Martha Nussbaum, and feminists Julia Kristeva and Luce Irigaray are writing, why have I chosen to write about five dead white males? This is truly a just question, and one that requires a reflective response. The philosophers I have chosen had extraordinary opportunities (Gladwell, 2008)† to study and to think that have, until very recently, been unthinkable for women. Each of them had a wife who supported him and raised their children. Each stood on the shoulders of philosophical giants, male philosophers like Plato, Descartes, Kant, and even Heidegger. Unlike the women of any generation so far, they had the chance to become the great philosophers who have inspired my own thinking and that of many others. In particular, they have provided philosophical resources for working clinicians, and I am very grateful for their lives and work.

But we women have a lot of catching up to do. As a young graduate student in philosophy, and as a tenure-track assistant professor of philosophy in the 1970s, I was nearly always the only woman. It was almost impossible to find one's way into any conversation, and the contempt of my male colleagues felt thick and heavy. Soon, also attracted by clinical work, I stepped off the tenure track to study clinical psychology and, later, psychoanalysis. I tell this story only because I imagine that many other women of my generation faced similar struggles, though clearly some survived, and many more women work in philosophy now. But I believe it will take generations before women have the opportunities and support to appear among the world's greatest philosophers. To me this is a great sorrow, and one that clouds the great pleasure I also take in studying the philosophers included in this book.

---

* Robert Stolorow, George Atwood, and I (in press) have also written an attempt to understand psychobiographically Heidegger's enthusiastic—and never revoked—support for the National Socialists.
† Note that no women appear in Gladwell's study of extraordinary achievers who had extraordinary opportunities.

DIALOGUES IN A HERMENEUTIC SPIRIT

This book attempts to enter and maintain dialogue on several levels: between philosophy and psychotherapy, psychoanalysis included; between theory and clinical practice; among the philosophers considered; implicitly, between the psychoanalytic traditions and those of our humanistic colleagues; between text and reader; and among the competing voices each of us hears. Each of these dialogues requires what I call a "hermeneutic sensibility." Most of all, such a hermeneutic attitude—the topic of a future book—makes our clinical work possible.

A hermeneutic therapeutic sensibility includes, to my mind, the following: (a) a strong sense of one's own situation—including one's theories, personal history, and personality organization—that constantly and inevitably shapes and limits both one's actual understanding and one's capacity to understand a particular patient; (b) a sense of experiential world or system, one's own, the patient's, and that formed with the patient; (c) a strong sense of complexity that resists all forms of reductionism and technical rationality in clinical work; (d) a sensitivity to the languages of personal experience, including their nonverbal backgrounds and forms of expression; (e) a strong developmental-historical sense that gives, overall, equal emphasis to past and future, one that attends to processes of emergence, including emergence of defense and dissociation, throughout the clinical process; (f) a belief that understanding is effective, that is, that understanding in the rich sense is curative; (g) a conviction that dialogue and conversation are the best way to create and register that emotional resonance indispensable to meaning-oriented work; and (h) a sense of vocation and devotion similar to Friedrich Schleiermacher's "rigorous practice." For Schleiermacher, "misunderstanding occurs as a matter of course, and so understanding must be willed and sought at every point" (Schleiermacher, 1998, p. 110). It is my hope that these components of a hermeneutic sensibility pervade the whole book and create a climate of welcome to the many conversations.

2

MARTIN BUBER
The Dialogic We

A soul is never sick alone.

—Buber

The wounds of the order-of-being can be healed in infinitely many other places than those at which they were inflicted.

—Buber

The contribution of Martin Buber (1878–1965), philosopher of dialogue, inclusion, and confirmation, has gone largely unnoticed in the psychoanalytic world.* On the other hand, his work has been warmly welcomed by the communities of humanistic psychotherapists, especially earlier, by Carl Rogers in the 1950s, and more recently, by gestalt therapists (Yontef, 1988; Hycner & Jacobs, 1995). They have seen in his philosophy of the I-Thou encounter a therapeutic ideal of healing through person-to-person contact and through what they, following Buber, call confirmation.

How can we explain this difference? First, as we can see in Buber's correspondence (Buber, 1991, 1999), he challenged both Freud and Jung, finding them wanting. Freud, he believed, was too reductionist and mechanistic, too inclined to reify the unconscious, and too dismissive of religious experience (Buber, 1999). Freud had considered real guilt as if it were merely neurotic, thus precluding actual reconciliation (Buber,

---

* Notable exceptions appear in the work of relational psychoanalysts Darlene Ehrenberg (1992) and Lewis Aron (1996).

1948). Freud saw love as instinctual response to something missing, where Buber thought of love as abundant and generous, "a voluntary process of witnessing, affirming, bestowing a sense of worth and recognition on other, analogous to gift-giving" (Burston & Frie, 2006, p. 166).

In his turn Jung had claimed that he studied only the "facts" of human nature and concluded from these "that all statements about God have their origin in the psyche" (Buber, 1999, p. 65), leading Buber to rejoin: "These are not legitimate assertions of a psychologist who as such has no right to declare what exists beyond the psychic and what does not" (p. 68). Buber's form of humanism and of nondogmatic religion found much greater welcome among existentially oriented psychiatrists in Europe like Binswanger (Binswanger, 1942; Frie, 2003) and Hans Trüb (Buber, 1991a) as well as among humanistically oriented Americans (Friedman, 1994; Rogers, 1961; Buber, 1999). Psychoanalysts stopped listening.

This chapter will suggest that this loss is worth some recovery work. After a brief look at Buber's life and work, we will engage those of his ideas that have been so influential in the humanistic psychotherapies—I-You, dialogue, inclusion, and confirmation—and show how helpful they could be to contemporary relational and intersubjective systems psychoanalysis. We will conclude by considering the ethical challenge that Buber's thought poses for all of us involved with devastated human beings.

LIFE AND WORK

Martin Buber was born in Vienna in 1878, into a world of culture both grand and innovative in literature, music, science, philosophy, psychology, art, and architecture. It was a world in which Jews were not only demeaned—Freud could not hope for a professorship, for example— but also were making significant contributions, for example Freud, Wittgenstein, Arthur Schnitzler, Gustav Mahler, Stefan Zweig (Janik & Toulmin, 1973). It was also a world from which all these luminaries, if they lived into the *Nazizeit*, had to depart. Martin Buber—whose parents separated in 1882—departed much sooner, to grow up in Poland with his paternal grandparents, with whom he was very close and from whom he learned his love for languages and literature. As a young man, not knowing what he wanted to do or become, he studied literature, philosophy, and some psychology in Vienna, Leipzig, Berlin, and Zurich. First Nietzsche and later Kant were crucial philosophical influences (his writings in the history of philosophy were published posthumously, in 1948, as *Das Problem des Menschen*). In 1900, he moved to Berlin with his future wife Paula Winkler and became involved with early Zionism. He moved again in 1904 to Frankfurt to work with Franz Rosenzweig* (Rosenzweig, 1921/2005) and to fill a lectureship in Jewish religious studies and ethics at the university. There he became involved in publishing and remained in the Frankfurt area until 1937 when the family emigrated to Jerusalem, where he taught at Hebrew University. His writings in religious studies and philosophy—*I and Thou* (Buber, 1923/1970), *Tales of the Hasidim* (Buber, 1947/1991b)—made him a revered figure consulted by people from around the world, as his correspondence (Buber, 1991a) shows.

Buber was reticent about his private life but furnished a series of "autobiographical fragments" for the volume of the *Library of Living Philosophers* devoted to him (Schilpp, Friedman, & Buber, 1967). Of these, the first, from the age of 3 years, may be the most interesting to us analysts and therapists:

> The house in which my grandparents lived had a great rectangular inner courtyard surrounded by a wooden balcony extending to the roof on which one could walk around the building at each floor. Here I stood once in my fourth year with a girl several years older, the daughter of a neighbor, to whose care my grandmother had entrusted me. We both leaned on the railing. I cannot remember that I spoke of my mother to my older comrade. But I hear still how the big girl said to me, "No, she will never come back." I know that I remained silent, but also that I cherished no doubt of the truth of the spoken words. It remained fixed in me; from year to year it cleaved ever more to my heart, but after more than ten years I had begun to perceive it as something that concerned not only me, but all men. Later I once made up the word "*Vergegnung*"—"mismeeting," or "miscounter"—to designate the failure of a real meeting between men.[†] When after another twenty years I again saw my mother, who had come from a distance to visit me, my wife, and my children, I could not gaze into her still astonishingly beautiful eyes without hearing from somewhere the word "*Vergegnung*" as a word spoken to me. I suspect that all that I have learned about genuine meeting in the course of my life had its first origin in that hour on the balcony. (pp. 3–4)

It is possible to read each philosopher in this book as responding to traumatic losses and searching for ways to give them his own kind of sense, as Buber did here.

---

* A crucial influence on both Buber and Levinas (Rosenzweig & Galli, 2005).

† Translators usually render Buber's *Mensch* and *Menschen* as *man* and *men* in English, but the German word has a much more inclusive sense, more like *people*.

I AND THOU

The centerpiece of Martin Buber's philosophy—he called it his "believing humanism"—is a personally intimate encounter or meeting between I and Thou, which differs radically from all I-It relations, in which we regard the other as a thing. Unfortunately, translating Buber's *Ich-Du* as I-Thou creates and perpetuates a false impression, as Kaufmann (Buber, 1923/1970) explained in the preface to his translation. *Du* is the intimate form of *you*, used with lovers, children, and very close friends. *Thou*, instead, implies that the other is some kind of transcendent deity. For Buber, even when addressing deity, we use the *Du*.*

But what is this intimate dialogic contact, and why does it matter for our work? For Buber there are two basic words: I-You and I-It. Not only the second part differs: "The I of the basic word I-You is different from that in the basic word I-It" (Buber, 1923/1970, p. 53). How we stand in relation to the other changes us. In the I-It relation we can stand above or outside as observer, investigator, or artist (Buber, 1965). When, however, we allow the other to speak to us, something very different occurs:

> This person is not my object; I have got something to do with him. Perhaps I have something in him to complete; but perhaps I have only something to learn, and it only comes about that I "assume." Maybe I immediately have to answer this person; maybe speech would involve a long, complex transmission, and I must answer somewhere else, some other time, to someone else, in who knows what sort of language, and it comes about that I take the answer into myself. But a word happened to me† that demands an answer. (p. 152, translation mine)‡

Buber's other, his *Du*, is not part of me, but speaks into me as I do into him or her. Meeting the other as a *Du* changes us both by the word that is spoken. But this relation has also a double character: It is our original condition and also a surprise, the given and the unexpected.

---

* For me it is ironic, once we understand the intimacy of the therapeutic encounter (healing through meeting, according to Buber's friend, Hans Trueb, 1952), that so many psychoanalysts continue to insist on formal forms of address (in German, *Sie*; in French, *vous*; in Italian, *Lei*; in English, *Mr.* or *Ms.*) between analysts and patients.

† The Hebrew/Semitic *dabar* is both *word* and *thing, occurrence*. Once uttered, a *dabar* is considered an objective thing. It cannot be unspoken. It is claimed, for example, that Moses often heard the *dabar* of the biblical deity (I owe this observation to D. Braue and to *Langenscheidt*'s Hebrew/English Dictionary, 1961).

‡ In this passage the word of the other person much resembles Levinas's "face of the other" that places an infinite responsibility on me. We will see that Gadamer says something similar.

As original condition, I-You is primal. To support this view, Buber (1923/1970) cited the Zulu single sentence-word: "Mother, I am lost," and the tribal Fuegian sentence-word of seven syllables: "They look at each other, each waiting for the other to offer to do that which both desire but neither wishes to do" (p. 70). Buber inferred from these kinds of expressions that "in this wholeness persons are still embedded like reliefs without achieving the fully rounded independence of nouns or pronouns. What counts is not these products of analysis and reflection but the genuine original unity, the lived relationship" (p. 70). The primary word I-You "splits into I and You, but it did not originate as their aggregate, it antedates any I" (p. 74). Because of this primacy, he claims, "the longing for relation is primary, the cupped hand into which the being that confronts us nestles; and the relation to that which is a wordless anticipation of saying You, comes second" (p. 78).

Buber does not suggest that we can live exclusively in the I-You. Instead, this relation exists as latency much more commonly than as a moment of experience. In the words of Lynne Jacobs (personal communication, October 20, 2008),

> the I-Thou attitude (so obvious with a good teacher or therapist), interpenetrates the highly valuable discussion of content that is in the I-It realm. It is the interpenetration that makes the I-It meaningful, useable, I believe. And evil is a consequence of alienation from the world of I-Thou as a possibility.

If relation is our original condition, when it goes wrong—as Buber's own life attests—then the longing for relation can shape our lives in compelling ways. In relational psychoanalysis, especially in intersubjective systems theory (Orange, Atwood, & Stolorow, 1997; Stolorow et al., 1987), persons are always already embedded in relational contexts that may be more or less meetings in Buber's sense. Traumatic relational experience—"mismeetings," in Buber's language—creates fears and longings described and studied by attachment researchers who can see even the most "difficult" child as "leaning out for love" (Karen, 1994).

Although Buber's relation is primary—not at all the developmental achievement of mutual recognition studied by psychoanalytic Hegelians (Aron, 1996; Benjamin, 1995)—it also involves elements of surprise. We should expect to be caught unawares because this other person is not part of me:

> The actual other who meets me meets me in such a way that my soul comes in contact with his as with something that it is not and that it cannot become. My soul does not and cannot include the

other, and yet can approach the other in this most real contact. (Buber, 1999, p. 56)

And again, speaking of the "personal making present" necessary for true contact, Buber wrote:

> The chief presupposition for the rise of genuine dialogue is that each should regard his partner as the very one he is. I become aware of him, aware that he is different, essentially different from myself, in the definite, unique way which is peculiar to him, and I accept whom I thus see, so that in full earnestness I can direct what I say to him as the person he is. (pp. 79–80)

We should thus expect that there will be disagreements, misunderstandings, and surprises, familiar to all of us in our work. In fact, Buber believed surprise was an essential element of the dialogic encounter between I and You, and therefore cautioned against reliance on method and theory in psychotherapy. He spoke with members of the Washington School of Psychiatry in 1957:

> The usual therapist imposes himself on the patient without being aware of it. . . . the therapist approaches the patient, but he must try to influence him as little as possible, that is the patient must not be influenced by the general ideas of the school [of thought]. The patient must be left to himself, if I may say so, with the humility of the master, and then the therapist awaits the unexpected and does not put what comes into categories. . . . It is much easier to impose than to use the whole force of the soul to leave him to himself and not to touch him, so to speak. (Buber, 1999, p. 240)

We find, thus, that reading Buber can imbue us psychoanalysts with a less "knowing" attitude than that encouraged by traditional psychoanalysis. (I remember being told by a supervisor that a competent and experienced psychoanalyst is never surprised). Instead, Buber wrote to Ludwig Binswanger that "dialogue in my sense implies the necessity of the unforeseen, and its basic element is surprise, the surprising mutuality" (Buber, 1999, p. 190). Although Daniel Stern's recent work (2004) does not mention Buber, his description of present moments with their unexpected quality and full mutuality, dependent always on preexisting processes of intersubjective mutual regulation, might have been congenial to Buber. Likewise, Buber might have been charmed by Winnicott's (1971) dialogic courting of surprise in the squiggle game. Reverent toward the other, holding our theories lightly (Orange, 1995), and remaining ready for the surprising encounter with the You, we look every hour for the You to be met in our work.

But this often means working in the dark, in worlds of traumatic devastation, uncertainty (Brothers, 2008), personal risk (Jaenicke, 2008), loneliness, and loss. The dialogic path is risky:

> The basic word can only be spoken with one's whole being; whoever commits himself may not hold back part of himself; and the work does not permit me, as a tree or man might, to seek relaxation in the It-world; it [both word and work?] is imperious: if I do not serve it properly, it breaks, or it breaks me (Buber, 1923/1970, pp. 60–61).

Without so many assumptions, categories, methods of observations, and the like to protect us, we are like the pilgrims in one of Buber's early religious works: "No way can be pointed to in this desert night. We can only help others to stand fast in readiness, until the dawn breaks and a path becomes visible where none suspected it" (quoted by Helmut Kuhn in Schilpp et al., 1967, p. 647). This attitude resembles the radical hope described by Jonathan Lear (2006), the only possibility in the face of some kinds of cultural or personal devastation (Orange, 2008a).

Still, this attitude is not mystical. In 1957 Buber wrote an afterword to *I and Thou* (originally published in 1923), responding to some questions put to him over the years. "The clear and firm structure of the I-You relationship, familiar to anyone with a candid heart and courage to stake it, is not mystical.* To understand it we must sometimes step out of our habits of thought, but not out of the primal norms" (1923/1970, p. 177). Speaking of I-You relatedness to the natural world, he notes that

> our habits of thought make it difficult for us to see that . . . something [the *dabar*, the word] is awakened by our attitude and flashes toward us from that which has being. What matters . . . is that we should do justice with an open mind to the actuality of what opens up before us. (p. 173)

For Buber, the natural attitude[†] is one that does not reduce the other to an It.

Having claimed that relation is reciprocity, Buber (1923/1970) was also often asked whether the I-You meeting had to be entirely reciprocal.

---

* For a history of Jewish mysticism, see Scholem (1995). Buber—who seems to have thought mysticism was fusion or communion—may also have been responding here to criticism from Levinas, who learned from Buber but found his account of relation too religious, too "mystical," and worst of all, too reciprocal. See Chapter 5.
† This is not the "natural attitude" of founder of phenomenology Edmund Husserl (The Hague, 1913/1982), who saw the natural attitude as the whole collection of everyday and scientific assumptions that we need to put aside (bracket) in order to describe "the things themselves" experientially or phenomenologically.

Even if I approach the other nonreductionistically, turning toward the You, as Buber often said, I may offer the "great gift" in vain: "Everything tells you that complete mutuality does not inhere in men's life with one another. It is a form of grace for which one must always be prepared but on which one can never count" (p. 178). He also believed that some I-You relationships—teacher-student, therapist-patient, and spiritual leader-congregant—"by their very nature may never unfold into complete mutuality if they are to remain faithful to their nature" (p. 178). The helping relationship is asymmetrical by nature (Buber, 1999), even when the helper approaches the other as a You, because the therapist's true task,

> the regeneration of a stunted personal center . . . can be brought
> off only by a man who grasps with the profound eye of a physician
> the buried, latent unity of the suffering soul, which can be done
> only if he enters as a partner in a person-to-person relationship,
> but never through the observation and investigation of an object
> . . . the therapist, like the educator, must stand not only at his own
> pole of the bipolar relationship but also at the other pole, experi-
> encing the effects of his own actions. (p. 179)*

The healing relationship ends when the patient tries to experience from the healer's vantage point, in Buber's view. To me it seems that these healing-and-teaching relationships share the indispensable asymmetry of parenting. Buber implies that making parents (Burston & Frie, 2006) of our children, students, or patients shifts them from You to It, making them parentified objects to meet our needs.

So the I-You relation need not be constant, cannot always be fully reciprocal, and is not mystical. It is, however, intimate, surprising, risky, and creates a genuine We. The word (*dabar*) that arises between I and You comes to life in the We of speech, "the communal speaking that begins in the midst of speaking to one another" (Buber, 1999, p. 106). The We, the living community of the past and present, depends on language, always ontologically present

> wherever one communicated to the other his own experience
> in such a way that it penetrated the other's circle of experience
> and supplemented it from within, so that from now on his per-
> ceptions were set within a world as they had not been before. All
> this flowing ever again into a great stream of reciprocal sharing of

---

* Of course there are many other conceptions of intersubjectivity in philosophy and in contemporary psychoanalysis. The one on which intersubjective systems theory relies I might call primary intersubjectivity, the field or system into which each of us is born and in which our personal experiential world takes form.

knowledge—thus came to be and thus is the living We, the genuine We, which, where it fulfills itself, embraces the dead who once
took part in colloquy and now take part in it through what they
have handed down to posterity. (p. 107)

For Buber this *We* was just as resistant to reduction to the third person as is the I and the You. This *We* "is no collective, no group, no objec-
tively exhibitable multitude" (p. 107). Like Heidegger (1927/1962), Buber
believed that the world is no collection of items. Unlike Heidegger,
Buber saw the *We* as composed of the very particular and personal I
and You embedded in further relation to the *We* of tradition and language. Philosopher of dialogue, Buber accused Dasein's "solicitude"*
of being "monological" and enclosed: "In Heidegger's world there is no
such *Thou*, no true *Thou* spoken from being to being, spoken with one's
own being. One does not say this *Thou* to the man for whom one is
merely solicitous" (Buber, 1947/2002, p. 204).

Language, Buber believed, is essentially dialogic. Even the internal
monologue, the "inner word," the dialogue with oneself, "is possible
only because of the basic fact of men's speaking with each other" (Buber,
1988, p. 102). It is currently fashionable to consider the "implicit" as a
separate realm of being; I think Buber would have strongly disagreed.
He thought we often notice that we have got hold of something "without meeting a word," but then we notice it "striving toward language"
(Buber, 1999, p. 149). "In speaking the inner word he does not want to
be heard by himself, for he knows it already as the person uttering it.
Rather he wants to be heard by the nameless, unconceived, inconceivable
other, by whom he wants to be understood in his having understood"
(p. 150). Buber implied that Descartes and his followers—"de-Socratizing philosophers"—have lost the Socratic dialogic context and fallen
into a "monologizing hubris." Granted, this inner dialogue still lacks
something—the other, the moment of surprise: "The human person is
not in his own mind unpredictable to himself as he is to any one of his
partners: therefore, he cannot be a genuine partner to himself, he can be
no real questioner and no real answerer" (p. 150). The word "becomes
fruitful where, out of understanding each other, genuine dialogue

---

* Heidegger's (1927/1962) *Sorge*, often translated "solicitude" or "care," characterizes
human being-with: "Dasein's resoluteness towards itself is what first makes it possible to
let the other who are with it 'be' in their ownmost potentiality-for-Being, and to co-dis-
close this potentiality in the solicitude which leaps forth and liberates. Only by authentically Being-Their-Selves in resoluteness can people authentically be with one another" (p.
298). Even sympathetic critics like Vogel (1994) find Heidegger's "other" less than a You
in Buber's sense, let alone the other of the face in Levinas (see Chapter 5). Buber discussed
and criticized Heidegger extensively in Buber (1999).

unfolds" (p. 150). Such a spoken word is always ambiguous, having an "aura" (p. 151); the dialogic word may even be a silent sitting or walking together (p. 258). Like the other philosophers we will study, Buber recognizes that the words we speak to each other differ fundamentally from the reductionistic "without remainder" language of science.

INCLUSION

A second concept crucial to Buber's dialogic philosophy and especially dear to gestalt therapists, is inclusion (*Umfassung*).* His meaning is difficult to explain. By inclusion he did not mean inclusiveness exactly, though his thought was surely inclusive. He considered not just his own tradition but also studied many European languages and the literatures of Asian religions (Buber, 1957; Buber & Friedman, 1988; Friedman, 2002). Nor did he mean empathy, which for him meant leaving oneself and sliding over into the other as an object, "as it were, to trace it from within" (Buber, 1947/2002, pp. 114–115). Empathy, he claimed, "means the exclusion of one's own concreteness, the extinguishing of the actual situation of life, the absorption in pure aestheticism of the reality in which one participates" (p. 115).† Empathy for him suggested a mystical or aesthetic intuitionism, a neglect of the actual You and of the actual Between or interhuman (*das Zwischenmenschliche*). So inclusion is not *Einfühlung* (empathy), feeling one's way into the other's life experience.

Instead, what he meant by inclusion was a particular feature of I-You relating, the "opposite" of empathy:

> It is the extension of one's own concreteness, the fulfillment of the actual situation of life, the complete presence of the reality in which one participates. Its elements are, first a relation, of no matter what kind, between two persons, second, an event experienced by them in common, in which at least one of them actively participates, and third, the fact that this one person, without forfeiting anything of the felt reality of his activity, at the same time lives through the common event from the standpoint of the other. (Buber, 1947/2002, p. 115)

For Buber, such relating is not mystical (in the sense of absorption in the other) but is a concrete encounter between two persons. When

---

* This German word has the meanings of inclusion, and especially of embracing. Buber usually means both.

† Intersubjective systems theorists (Stolorow, Atwood, & Orange, 2002) have similarly criticized the notion of "empathic immersion" used by some self psychologists.

an I and a You experience an event together, the experience of the one comes to include the standpoint of the other.* In the clinical situation, for example, I as the eldest of 10 children must work very hard to include the experience of younger or only children in my reality. I must, to use Buber's expression, extend my own concreteness. When a patient who had been a younger child says to me that he cannot understand how any woman would not be fascinated by him, how she could possibly walk away, my immediate, noninclusive impulse could be to call him a terminal narcissist. Only when I, "without forfeiting anything" of my own experience, stretch toward—Buber would say "turn toward"—the other can I begin to understand the multiple possible meanings for the patient. Perhaps his parents, thrilled to have a child after losing everyone in the Holocaust, were endlessly and anxiously fascinated by him. Or perhaps his parents were emotionally absent, or inconsistent, to the extent that the child—later my patient—could never understand why the parents showed interest in their first child but not in him. He still does not understand and is terrified by noninterest. There are many other possible meanings. Buber's point seems close to that of intersubjective systems theorists who likewise believe we experience or live through common events in a world we coinhabit. We reach for meaning and healing through dialogic inclusion of the other's perspective in our own, and by way of our own. Once again, "The basic word I-You can only be spoken with one's whole being. The basic word I-It can never be spoken with one's whole being" (Buber, 1923/1970, p. 54). So the work of inclusion is the work of "making present." I imagine what the other is "at this very moment wishing, feeling, perceiving, thinking, and not as a detached content" but in the living process of this person (Buber, 1999, p. 14). This is not vague sympathy, but an

> event in which I experience . . . the specific pain of another in such a way that I feel what is specific in it, not, therefore a general discomfort or state of suffering, but this particular pain as the pain of the other. This making present increases until it is a paradox in the soul when I and the other are embraced by a common living situation, and . . . the pain which I inflict upon him surges up in myself . . . at such a moment something can come into being which cannot be built up in any other way. (Buber, 1999, pp. 14–15)

---

* Gadamer (1960/1991) speaks quite similarly of the fusion of horizons (*die Horizontverschmelzung*), and I have written about perspectival realism, in which the conversation of perspectives creates the possibility of understanding more than would be possible from a single perspective but does not involve abandoning one's own situated point of view (Orange, 1995).

To understand what Buber means, let us consider the following clinical situation. My patient has told me, with some trepidation, of a sexual incident about which he doubts the wisdom of his own participation. I respond with concern, fearing that my patient is endangering himself (i.e., could contract AIDS). The patient returns the following week, feeling judged and rejected and shamed by me. "I always thought you were on my side," he laments, "and now I don't know." Since I thought my response had been only protective and concerned, I am faced with the work of inclusion. My patient's reality is a specific pain that has little to do with the unprotected sex. As we explore the dashed hope that he had finally met someone who could simply accompany, understand, and support him, and as we travel down the horrible spirals of relationally generated shame, his pain becomes real and present to me until we are "embraced by a common living situation." *Umfassung* means both inclusion and embrace.

This is why Buber speaks of inclusion as a form of participation (*Dabeisein*).* Wilhelm Dilthey, Buber's philosophy teacher in Berlin, had seen the objectivizing methods of the *Naturwissenschaften* (physical sciences) as inadequate to understanding (*Verstehen*) in the humanities or *Geisteswissenschaften*. Similarly, Buber contrasted the observing approach with the participatory or inclusive attitude needed to know the other. Though Plato had spoken of knowledge as participation in the Ideas, Buber thought knowledge through inclusion meant participation in the human situation with the other. "The two participate in one another's lives in very fact, not psychically but ontically" (Buber, 1947/2002, p. 170). This could be confusing for those of us who have learned from Heidegger to distinguish the *ontological* (thinking about being-in-the-world) from the *ontic* (talking about the beings that we count and measure). By *ontically,* Buber seems to have meant in their whole being, as required for speaking the basic word I-You.†

The path of inclusion is a hard, dark, and rocky one. In a small memorial piece for his friend the Swiss psychotherapist Hans Trüb (1952), Buber wrote that "a soul is never sick alone, but there is always

---

* Buber's *Dabeisein* has connotations both of participation and of presence in German.

† Levinas thought *Umfassung*, or inclusion, "one of the most original notions of [Buber's] philosophy. . . . The I in its relation with the Thou is further related to itself by means of the Thou, i.e., it is related to the Thou as to someone who in turn relates itself to the I, as though it had come into delicate contact with himself through the skin of the Thou. It thus returns to itself by means of the Thou. This relation should be distinguished from the psychological phenomenon of *Einfühlung* [empathy] where the subject puts itself completely in the other's place, thus forgetting itself. In the case of *Einfühlung*, the I forgets itself, and does not feel itself as thou of the Thou, whereas in the *Umfassung* the I sharply maintains its active reality" (Schilpp et al., 1967, p. 142).

a between-ness also, a situation between it and another existing being" (Buber, p. 21), even though one feels so alone.

Explaining to Buber why, in spite of many positive experiences, he could not write his book, Trüb described himself as having the "tunnel disease" of people who always work underground:

> I have under great renunciation of the spiritual general context, reached the lonely and hidden place of the isolated persons—hoping for the best, if I ever find my way back—and now that I really can communicate with the single, isolated individual, I don't find my way back. I am afraid of indiscretion. I avoid the light of day and am frightened of my own word. (p. 171)

Healing through meeting, as both Buber and Trüb called it, or working in the interhuman, is perilous for both healer (cf. Jaenicke, 2008) and patient. In Buber's words, "It is a cruelly hazardous enterprise, this becoming a whole" (Buber, 1999, p. 26). As we saw before, he spoke of the human speaker of the I-You word as undertaking sacrifice and risk: "The basic word . . . is imperious: if I do not serve it properly, it breaks, or it breaks me." (Buber, 1923/1970, p. 60–61)

CONFIRMATION

A central concept in gestalt therapy, Buber's confirmation could also be useful to relational psychoanalysis:

> Everything is changed in real meeting. Confirmation can be misunderstood as *static*. I meet another—I accept and confirm him as he now is. But confirming a person *as he is* is only the first step, for confirmation does not mean that I take his appearance at this moment as the person I want to confirm. I must take the other person in his dynamic existence, in his specific potentiality. How can I confirm what I want most to confirm in his present being? That is the hidden, for in the present lies hidden what *can become*. His potentiality makes itself felt to me as that which I would most confirm. (Buber, 1999, pp. 242–243)

Indispensable to the I-You relation is Buber's concept of confirmation, the most important effect of genuine inclusion. When I reach over into the life experience of the other to make the other present in his or her unique being, I seek to confirm that being as other, as You. If I relate to the other as an it, as something observed, as a content of my experience, "dialogue becomes a fiction, the mysterious intercourse between two human worlds only a game, and in the rejection of the real life confronting [me] the essence of all reality begins to disintegrate" (Buber,

1947/2002). Besides, Buber explained, we humans full of possibility need confirmation:

> Man as man is an audacity of life, undetermined and unfixed; he therefore requires confirmation, and he can naturally only receive this as individual man, in that others and he himself confirm him in his being-this-man. Again and again the Yes must be spoken to him, from the look of the confidant and from the stirrings of his own heart, to liberate him from the dread of abandonment, which is a foretaste of death. (Buber, 1999, p. 30)

But what exactly did he mean by "confirm"? I find no single definition in Buber's work, but a cluster of explanations:

1. "The other knows that he is made present by me in his self and . . . this knowledge induces the process of his inmost self-becoming" (Buber, 1999, p. 15).
2. "Man wishes to be confirmed in his being by man, and wishes to have a presence in the being of the other . . . sent forth from the natural domain of species into the hazard of the solitary category, surrounded by the air of a chaos which came into being with him, secretly and bashfully he watches for a Yes which allows him to be and which comes to him only from one human person to another. It is from one man to another that heavenly bread of self-being is passed" (p. 16).
3. "The speaker does not merely perceive the one who is present to him in this way [as a whole and unique being]; he receives him as his partner, and means that he confirms this other being, so far as it is for him to confirm. The true turning of his person to the other includes this confirmation, this acceptance. Of course, such a confirmation does not mean approval; but no matter in what I am against the other, by accepting him as my partner in genuine dialogue I have affirmed him as a person" (Buber, 1962, p. 86).

By *Bestätigung* (English: confirmation), Buber seems to mean something close to inclusion, but specifically acceptance as a partner in dialogue (*Gesprächspartner*), whether one expects to agree or not. The German word has the usual translations of confirmation, certification (e.g., of an official appointment), or acknowledgment. Thus it corresponds closely to Hegel's *Anerkennung*, recognition as someone of a particular status, the status of a dialogic partner. Thus Buber shifted the focus from subject-status to partner-status. Relation is primary.

What Buber did not mean by confirmation was approval. He considered actual (nonneurotic) guilt fundamental to the human condition, and confirmation includes the recognition of this real guilt. Guilt, he declared,

> is not hidden away inside the human person, but . . . the human person stands, in the most real way, in the guilt that envelops him . . . to understand the suppression of the knowledge of the guilt as a merely psychological phenomenon will not suffice. It hinders the guilty man, in fact, from accomplishing the reconciliation. (Buber, 1999, p. 19)

Indeed, in his essay "Guilt and Guilt Feelings" he described what he called "existential guilt"—personal guilt for personal misdeeds or omissions—and spoke of the burden that working with such guilt places on the healer:

> The doctor who confronts the effects on the guilty man of an existential guilt must proceed in all seriousness from the situation in which the act of guilt has taken place. Existential guilt occurs when someone injures an order of the human world whose foundations he knows and recognizes as those of his own existence and of all common human existence. The doctor who confronts such a guilt in the living memory of his patient must enter into that situation; he must lay his hand in the wound of the other and learn: this concerns you. But then it may strike him that the orientation of the psychologist and the treatment of the therapist have changed unawares and that if he wishes to persist as a healer he must take upon himself a burden he had not expected to bear. (Buber, 1999, p. 116)

Reading these words, I have been reminded of a Vietnam veteran with whom I worked about 25 years ago. He arrived at the clinic with a huge knife in his belt. My first task, admonished by my supervisors, was to persuade him that it would be safe enough to come to the clinic without a knife. Although the Veterans Administration had sent him to us with a "post-traumatic stress disorder" diagnosis, and of course, hoped that we could help them to cure his heroin addiction and explosiveness, I soon learned that my task more resembled what Buber had described. This man was tortured both by the memory of the atrocities he had committed and gloated over in Vietnam, and by the effects of his current behavior on his family. This was not a matter of removing neurotic guilt feelings, nor even of "shame-busting" though this would have become important had he survived (he died soon after from a drug overdose), but of allowing him to "lay my hand in the wound" he had inflicted on the human world. Such a burden, as Buber realized, never fully leaves the healer.

In less dramatic clinical work, we confirm the other every day by patiently working with people discouraged by circumstances and by their own patterned responses. The patient with a terminal illness, for example, who can see very little future, still seeks the connection with another human to confirm the value and dignity of a life that is slipping away, often further devalued by technological medicine.

Buber's confirmation emphasizes the personal and potential uniqueness of the actual person rather than the abstract status of subject. Confirmation seems to include much of what Kohutians mean by "mirroring" leading to the consolidation of self experience, and of what some relational psychoanalysts would mean by "recognition." But neither school of thought quite approaches Buber's saying Yes to the You with whom I am and will be in dialogic relation. Confirming, he told Carl Rogers, means "accepting the whole potentiality of the other and making even a decisive difference in his potentiality" (Buber, 1999, p. 266). This description of the psychotherapist's task resembles what we find in some psychoanalytic accounts of recognition, the profound recognition that creates new possibilities in the life of the suffering other (Eisold, 1999), or a kind of psychoanalytic compassion (Orange, 2006).

BUBER'S ANTIREDUCTIONISM

Buber's original contrast of the I-Thou relation with the I-It does not mean that I-It instrumental relations are avoidable. They constitute the bulk of our everyday being-in-the-world, to borrow Heidegger's language (1927/1962). But for Buber these everyday I-It interactions miss the meeting with the Thou or You. They reduce the other person or animal to an object of use, "without remainder."* In addition, he described the specifically modern approach as "an analytical, reductive and deriving [deducing] look between man and man" (Buber & Friedman, 1988, p. 70), reductive because

---

* Here is his account of clinical reductionism: "Consider, for example, the relation of doctor and patient. It is essential that this should be a real human relation experienced with the spirit by the one who is addressed; but as soon as the helper is touched by the desire—in however subtle a form—to dominate or to enjoy his patient, or to treat the latter's wish to be dominated or enjoyed by him other than as a wrong condition needing to be cured, the danger of a falsification arises, beside which all quackery appears peripheral" (Buber, 1947/2002, p. 113).

I think, without access to the original German, that by "enjoy" Buber meant "objectify" or perhaps "exploit" in this context.

it tries to contract the manifold person, who is nourished by the microcosmic richness of the possible, to some schematically surveyable and recurrent structures. And this look is a deriving one because it supposes it can grasp what man has become, or even is becoming, in genetic formulae, and it thinks that even the dynamic central principle of the individual in this becoming can be represented by a general concept. (pp. 70–71)

For Buber, however, the encounter that meets the unique person always resists such reduction. If I reduce the other though diagnosis or by any other form of experience-distant description—whether from psychology, sociology, or neuroscience—I have missed the encounter and objectified the other:

We have in common with all existing beings that we can be made objects of observation. But it is my privilege as man that by the hidden activity of my being I can establish an impassable barrier to objectification. Only in partnership can my being be perceived as an existing whole. (Buber, 1999, p. 75)

And again, "What the most learned and ingenious combination of concepts denies, the humble and faithful beholding, grasping, knowing of any situation bestows. The world is not comprehensible, but it is embraceable through the embracing of one of its beings" (quoted in Friedman, 1994, pp. 104–105). Only if we speak the I-You word to each other can we share a genuine human dialogue beyond all reductionisms.

For Buber, the originary I-You is irreducible to experience, theory, or knowledge. This irreducibility is not the incompressibility of the complexity theorists—though these different ideas seem compatible—but rather the I-You is unique, unrepeatable, and eludes definition.

BUBER AS HUMANIST

As we saw in the introduction, humanism has acquired a bad reputation in many quarters, for its alleged atheism, speciesism, and in the view of Heidegger, its allegiance to traditional metaphysics (Heidegger, 1967/1998). For Heidegger, his refusal of traditional Western metaphysics included a refusal to speak of ethics, the personal other, or of dialogue. Nevertheless, and knowing of all these objections, Martin Buber proclaimed himself a "believing humanist" (Atterton, Calarco, & Friedman, 2004; Buber, 1967). What could he have meant?

By "believing humanism," Buber seems to have meant something pretheoretical, not education-related (as in "the humanities"), and nonmetaphysical, what Calarco calls the common or philanthropic sense of humanism, "a joining of one's humanity with a certain ethics and faith, i.e., with a respect for the Other who is outside one's own scope of knowing" (Atterton et al., 2004, p. 253). Buber distinguished his "believing humanism" from the views of Hegel and Heidegger, who saw in the human the only full sense of Being or consciousness. In these views, according to Buber (1967), the essential human purpose is "reflexion [bending back on oneself], the reflection on oneself through which . . . [man] ever again accomplishes the reflection of *Being* on itself" (p. 118). (I might call these "narcissistic humanisms.") Buber inclusively escapes the charge of speciesism and simultaneously refuses the Heideggerian evasion of ethics, while accepting the Heideggerian location of the human as being-in-the-world, understood by Buber as being-in-relation. In Buber's own thinking,

> What appears here as the *humanum*, as the great superiority of man before all other living things known to us, is his capacity "of his own accord," hence not like the animals out of the compulsion of his needs and wants but out of the overflow of his existence, to come into direct contact with everything that he bodily or spiritually meets—to address it with lips and heart or even with the heart alone. (p. 119)

In other words, we are unique only in our capacity to say *Du* to the house cat, the oak tree, and to each other, not because we can objectify, reduce, and lord it over the others from the compulsion of our needs and wants. The human is an ethical relation that exceeds all knowing and using, all technological rationality, much as we will see that it does for Emmanuel Levinas (see Chapter 5).

But what besides an oxymoron could be a "believing humanism"? Any adequate response to this complex question would require a close examination of Buber's many religious texts, with special attention to his love for the Torah and for Hasidic stories and mysticism. But it would also attend to Buber's dialogic ethics, which led him—an exile from Nazi Germany and a 30-year resident of Jerusalem—to a concern for what the Palestinian people were suffering, and to a determination that their voices should be heard. His dialogic ethics further led him to an intense interest in the many ways that the ultimate *Du* is encountered, especially in the religions of Asia and the Middle East. We might say that Buber believed in the primacy of the I-You encounter, in any form this may take in various cultures, and that this pretheological faith (Hutchison, 1977) constituted his "believing humanism."

The ethical correlate of such a believing humanism is responsibility:* "Love is the responsibility of an I for a You" (Buber, 1923/1970, p. 66). Once again the *Du* can be surprisingly inclusive, as we find when we hear Buber's worries about the world situation: "Man will not persist in existence if he does not learn anew how to persist in it as a genuine We" (Buber & Friedman, 1988, p. 98). This is not exactly the ethics of equality and justice that comes down to us from Kant, more recently through Rawls (1971) and Habermas (1981/1984). Still, it shares something with Kant's second formulation of the categorical imperative: that we should treat each other as ends, not solely as means. The dialogic encounter with the other, the cornerstone of Buber's ethics, excludes exploiting each other, because the other is always also a potential *Du*. After an encounter with a troubled young man, he wrote:

> What do we expect when we are in despair and yet go to a man? Surely a presence by means of which we are told that nevertheless there is meaning.
>
> Since then I have given up the "religious" which is nothing but the exception, extraction, exaltation, ecstasy; or it has given me up. I possess nothing but the everyday out of which I am never taken. The mystery is no longer disclosed, it has escaped or it has made its dwelling here where everything happens as it happens. I know no fullness but each mortal hour's fullness of claim and responsibility. Though far from being equal to it, yet I know that in the claim I am claimed and may respond in responsibility, and know who speaks and demand a response.
>
> I do not know much more. If that is religion then it is just everything, simply all that is lived in its possibility of dialogue. (Schilpp et al., 1967, p. 26)

In subsequent chapters, we will encounter other views of dialogue, of the other, of ethics. We will encounter language-games, embodied intersubjectivity, hermeneutics, and the face of the other. Meanwhile we have met Buber's believing humanism of the primary word *Ich-Du*, and have been challenged never to be satisfied with the objectifying and reducing, if often inevitable, I-It. In our clinical work, Buber's inclusive humanism embraces us and inspires us in our work with those who have rarely if ever been really met within the interhuman.

---

* Levinas accused Buber—perhaps unjustly—of having underestimated the asymmetry of responsibility. See Chapter 5.

3

LUDWIG WITTGENSTEIN
Nothing Is Hidden

What we are supplying are really remarks on the natural history of human beings; we are not contributing curiosities, however, but observations which no one has doubted, but which have escaped remark only because they are always before our eyes.

—Wittgenstein

What we cannot speak about we must pass over in silence.

—Wittgenstein

Philosophy is a battle against the bewitchment of our intelligence by means of our language.

—Wittgenstein

Ludwig Wittgenstein (1889–1951) differs extensively but not profoundly from the other philosophers we consider in this book. His contributions to logic and to the ordinary-language philosophy that became the Anglo-American analytic school may seem to put him somewhat apart from the phenomenological humanism of Buber, Merleau-Ponty, Gadamer, and Levinas. But these differences may turn out to be more in style than substance. Wittgenstein, widely regarded—with Heidegger—as one of the two most influential 20th-century philosophers, relentlessly sought *clarity* just as others seek the good, indeed as others seek whatever god or gods they may believe in. Like Socrates, he epitomized the life and work of a philosopher—simple in style of life, publicity-avoiding, and challenging to received ideas and institutions. Convinced that philosophy—including logic—was truly an ethical task, Wittgenstein viewed working in philosophy as working on oneself—as a kind of therapy. Engaged in this therapy, he gave us several key ideas, and many more questions, that can protect us from—or at least warn us against—avoidable mistakes and blind assumptions in our clinical theory and practice. Once again, first, let us place Wittgenstein in his own life context.

LIFE AND WORK

Born in Vienna in 1889, Ludwig Wittgenstein was the youngest of eight children of Austrian steel magnate Karl Wittgenstein—of a Jewish family from Moravia—and of Leopoldine Wittgenstein, an Austrian Roman Catholic. Often compared to the Carnegies, the Wittgensteins lavishly patronized the arts. Their home is said to have contained nine grand pianos. Johannes Brahms was a frequent visitor, and his clarinet quintet was first performed in their home. The children were raised Catholic, schooled primarily at home in the sumptuous splendor of the Wittgenstein palace, and surrounded by music, as both parents were musical. Ludwig's brother Paul was a concert pianist who lost his right arm in World War I, and for whom several famous concertos for the left hand were written. Ludwig himself was known for his ability to whistle entire concertos flawlessly.

Their father, however, expected his sons to become engineers and to follow his own path into business. Three brothers died young from suicide, and suicide preoccupied Ludwig lifelong.* To his teacher, Bertrand Russell, and to his friends throughout life, he seemed mostly miserable. The sisters, one of whom became a patient of Freud, fared somewhat better, and Ludwig remained close with his sisters, especially Hermine.

Initially Ludwig attempted to follow the path of science and engineering, both in Berlin and in England. Gradually, however, he became fascinated with new developments in mathematical logic and sought out renowned logician Gottlob Frege, who advised him to go to Cambridge to study with Bertrand Russell, who—with Alfred North Whitehead—had just published *Principia Mathematica*. Russell was quite amazed by his tormented young student, whom he described as "passionate, profound, intense, and dominating" (Russell, 1968, vol. 2, p. 136).

---

* Like many young Viennese, Wittgenstein was much impressed by the views of duty and genius to be found in Weininger (1906). Weininger committed suicide in the house of Beethoven.

Already in 1912 Russell told Hermine Wittgenstein, visiting Ludwig in Cambridge, that "we expect the next big step in philosophy to be taken by your brother" (Rhees, 1984, p. 2). Though Russell mentored and supported him, Wittgenstein gradually lost respect for Russell as a thinker and became convinced that Russell understood nothing of his *Tractatus Logico-Philosophicus*. Worst of all, Russell seemed not to understand that the logical content of the *Tractatus* (what could be said) was unimportant next to the ethical (what could only be shown). "The whole sense of the book might be summed up in the following words," he began, "what can be said at all can be said clearly, and what we cannot talk about we must pass over in silence" (Wittgenstein, 1922/1974, p. 3).

Always discontent with academia and with academic philosophy and hoping for some kind of personal transformation, Wittgenstein joined the Austrian army during World War I, "the Great War," and during this time read and absorbed Tolstoy's *The Gospel in Brief*. In addition to his notebooks containing both personal (coded) and philosophical reflections, he produced his *Tractatus Logico-Philosophicus* (Wittgenstein, 2001), the only work he published in his lifetime. Here he gave a highly compressed account of relations between language and world. He then concluded that everything he had said about the restriction of meaningful propositions (the *gesagt*, or said) to those of natural science, though true, was trivial. The important aspects of human life, the mystical, could only be shown (*gezeigt*).

At the war's end, he was imprisoned for a year in Italy, where he read Kant and corresponded with people who might get his *Tractatus* published. Wittgenstein then distributed his inherited fortune to a few poets and mostly to his surviving siblings, and lived frugally. Cambridge philosopher David Ramsey, who visited Wittgenstein in the 1920s and ultimately lured him back to philosophy and to Cambridge in 1929, met Wittgenstein's family in Vienna. Puzzled by their apparent affection for one another together with Wittgenstein's adamant refusal to accept any monetary help from them, Ramsey suggested:

> it seems to be the result of a terribly strict upbringing. Three of his brothers committed suicide—they were made to work so hard by their father: at one time the eight children had twenty-six private tutors; and their mother took no interest in them. (quoted in Monk, 1990, p. 221)

Back in Vienna after the war, and rejected by the monastery he had wished to join, he became a dedicated but impatient schoolteacher in Austrian villages. Next he worked as a gardener and designed an extremely modern house for one of his sisters. Meanwhile, he had occasional visits from philosophers like Ramsey and conversation with members of the Vienna Circle, whose positivist misuses of his *Tractatus* Wittgenstein opposed then and later.

In 1929, already a celebrity, he was persuaded to return to Cambridge, where he received his doctorate for the *Tractatus* and where he lived and taught intermittently for the rest of his life. In Cambridge he began almost immediately to rethink his picture theory of language (where language represented the world a piece at a time), and to develop the meaning-as-use-in-context view we find in *Philosophical Investigations* and in all his later work. During World War II, unable to return to Austria because of his Jewish roots, he worked as a hospital orderly and later assisted in research on the care of those wounded by bombs. After the war he found teaching responsibilities increasingly unbearable. He thus sought the solitude needed for his thinking and writing in an isolated corner of Ireland, as he had done in Norway before World War I. Always torn, however, between needs for intense friendship and for quiet working conditions, he tended to move every few months. He died of cancer in Cambridge in 1951. He left *Philosophical Investigations* and an enormous German *Nachlass* (literary remains), from which his friends and colleagues have translated and published several volumes, large and small.

READING WITTGENSTEIN

Wittgenstein's favorite form of thinking and writing was dialogic.* He would spend long hours walking with a friend, saying: "Ask me a question." He would then engage with the presuppositions, grammatical confusions, and "temptations" involved in the question. Similarly his writings—always aphoristic in style and usually presented as numbered "remarks"—take the form of internal dialogues in which it may be difficult to distinguish a voice that simply belongs to Ludwig Wittgenstein. Often there seem to be more questions than answers (as in our own clinical work). For the sake of readers who

---

* "What reminds one, perhaps, most of Socrates in Wittgenstein [in addition to the dialogic style] are the patience and persistence with which he pursues his questions. Unhurried and yet relentless, both of them tease and harry the problems that concern them, hunting them down into their most hidden caves and corners. No question is too small for them, no trial too insignificant to pursue. Tirelessly they come back, again and again, to what preoccupies them. Profoundly concerned with the very words into which we have cast our philosophical predicaments, they will never lose sight of the great issues that lie behind them" (Sluga, 1996a, p. 30).

might want to read his work for themselves, here is an example from the *Philosophical Investigations*:*

> 560. "The meaning of a word is what is explained by the expla- nation of the meaning," i.e., if you want to understand the use of the word "meaning," look for what are called "explanations of meaning."
>
> 561. Now isn't it queer that I say that the word "is" is used with two different meanings (as the copula† and as the sign of equality), and should not care to say that its meaning is its use; its use, that is, as the copula and the sign of equality?
>
> One would like to say that these two kinds of use do not yield a *single* meaning; the union under one head is an accident, a mere inessential.
>
> 562. But how can I decide what is an essential, and what an ines- sential, accidental, feature of the notation? Is there some reality lying behind the notation, which shapes its grammar?
>
> Let us think of a similar case in a game: in draughts [checkers] a king is marked by putting one piece on top of another. Now won't one say it is inessential to the game for a king to consist of two pieces?

And so it goes. The quotation marks in 560 usually indicate that this is something others—especially confused philosophers—might say. It points up the initial need for philosophical therapy. Next, in 561, he muses about the oddness (*Merkwürdigkeit*) of the equivocal use of *is*, and asks whether one of these meanings is the real meaning and the other derived or nonessential. Still, it remains unclear whether these questions are his own or belong to another, somewhat confused inter- locutor. Next the sentence that begins, "One would like to say . . ." brings another possible—but probably also confused—solution to the double use of *is*. It is important to keep in mind that expressions like "one would like to say" or "one is tempted to say" usually indicate opin- ions with which Wittgenstein had some sympathy but which he was also convinced mislead us. Next, in 562, come the questions, still usu- ally representing confused ways of thinking—grammatical mistakes, he would have said—about the matter at hand. Finally comes the con- sideration of words as pieces in language-games played according to rules, a crucially important part of Wittgenstein's view of meaning as

---

* Wittgenstein is normally cited by work and paragraph number. Thus "1953, 650" means *Philosophical Investigations*, paragraph 650.

† *Copula* here refers to the grammatical uses of the verb 'to be,' as in "the rose is red," where rose and red are not equal.

use (in contexts). Almost any Wittgensteinian text can be read in this way, keeping in mind that often—as at the end of a clinical session—there will be no clear resolution of the matter under consideration. "You must bear in mind that the language-game is so to say something unpredictable. I mean: it is not based on grounds. It is not reasonable (or unreasonable). It is there—like our life" (Wittgenstein, 1953, 554; 1969). Doing philosophy is working on oneself, clearing up confusions that result from the temptation to take words as always having the same meanings. Without any appeal to unconsciousness, we begin to discuss with ourselves what we find ourselves saying.

MEANING AS USE IN A LANGUAGE-GAME

According to Wittgenstein, situation creates meaning. From the textual example above, we begin to gain a sense of this. His constant concern was with contexts of meaning, systems of communication (Wittgenstein, 1969), and grammar. By "grammar" he meant, not the conjugations, declensions, and parts of speech one studies in school or when learning a second language, but the whole of the language and what meanings a particular language permits without degenerating into nonsense. The grammar tells us whether there is any sense whatsoever in thinking of a king as two pieces stacked one atop the other. Only within the contexts of chess or checkers, including the rules of these games, does the use these games make of "king" have sense or meaning. There is no essence of kingness.

Shifting for a moment to our clinical preoccupations, let us ask about meaning in theoretical discourse in psychoanalysis and in other humanistic psychotherapies. Only in particular psychotherapeutic language-games, played according to their emergent but agreed-upon rules, do expressions like "internal object" (object relations theory) or "selfobject" (self psychology) or "contact" (gestalt therapy) have meaning. This holism or contextualism also becomes pragmatic because the meaning as use can be determined only in practical contexts.* Even the meaning of a smile depends on the situation:

> I see a picture which represents a smiling face. What do I do if I take the smile now as a kind one, now as malicious? Don't I often imagine it with a spatial and temporal context which is one either of kindness or malice? Thus I might supply the picture with the fancy that the smiler was smiling down on a child at play, or again on the suffering of an enemy. (Wittgenstein, 1953, 539)

---

* Here we may find an idea that overlaps with the early Heidegger's insistence that the everyday worlds of *Zuhandenheit* are the primordial sources of meaning.

Just as only within a particular sentence or paragraph can I determine whether *is* expresses copula or equality, we can only begin to understand the meanings of forms of politeness, or of expressions of suffering, within the culture to which they belong. As we will also see with Gadamer's hermeneutics, there is a continual back-and-forth between whole and parts in the search for meaning.

The most important whole in Wittgenstein's thought—and most useful for psychotherapeutic theory and practice, perhaps—is his already-mentioned "language-game" (*Sprachspiel*). For him, language-games, similar to games such as chess, are lived within cultures, or "forms of life." Just as in chess, where the game consists of the moves allowed to each piece, each language-game has its grammar, a set of rules that allow some locutions, and not others, to make sense. A language-game may be the brief orders and responses of construction workers, the language of a scientific discipline like chemistry or physics, the language of postmodern literary theory in which a language-game might be called a "discourse," the language of a particular school of psychotherapy or psychoanalysis, and so on. But these games also include much simpler matters that Wittgenstein found endlessly complex and formative of meanings: giving orders and obeying them, describing the appearance of an object or giving its measurements, reporting an event or speculating about an event, forming and testing a hypothesis, making up a story and reading it, play-acting, singing catches [rounds], guessing riddles, making and telling jokes, translating, requesting, thanking, cursing, greeting, praying (Wittgenstein, 1953, 23). Attention to the multiplicity of these languages keeps us alert to the complexity of meanings, and we are slower to assume that we know what the other person means. At the same time, familiarity with these games allows us to function in our worlds or forms of life with minimal hesitation.

Language-games themselves occur within what Wittgenstein called "this complicated form of life," available perhaps only to humans:

> One can imagine an animal angry, frightened, unhappy, happy, startled. But hopeful? And why not? A dog believes his master is at the door. But can he also believe his master will come the day after to-morrow?—And what can he *not* do here? . . . Can only those hope who can talk? Only those who have mastered the use of a language. That is to say, the phenomena of hope are modes of this complicated form of life. (1953, 148e)*

---

* The later sections of Wittgenstein, 1953 are referred to by page number, either German or English, for example, "p. 15g" or "p. 15e."

Though he was surely not the first to think humanness is in some way bound up with the capacity for language—if not limited to this capacity—Wittgenstein may have been the first philosopher to distinguish the human by our capacity to hope. Clearly he means something more complex that awaiting the arrival of food in the bowl, something more like Husserl's (1917/1964) phenomenology of internal time-consciousness. But for Wittgenstein language makes a language-game of hope possible—a fruitful thought, perhaps, for us clinicians.

The various language-games—well as the concepts to which these games give meaning—are related to each other, not by some shared essence, but by what Wittgenstein called "family resemblances," perhaps his second most famous idea. Any plurality, he thought, may share features, but complexly. In a family, for example, some members may have brown eyes, others may have curly hair, some faces may be round, and so on, but a stranger may look at a photo and say that these people are all related, even though no two members of the family share the same subset of the common characteristics. There is overlap, but no two members are even nearly identical. Claiming that his language-games share only these family resemblances, he exhorts:

> Consider for example the proceedings that we call "games." I mean board-games, card-games, ball-games, Olympic games, and so on. What is common to them all?—Don't say: "There must be something common, or they would not be called 'games'"—but *look and see* whether there is anything common to all.—For if you look at them you will not see something that is common to *all*, but similarities, relationships, and a whole series of them at that. To repeat: don't think, but look! (Wittgenstein, 1953, 66)

And the result of this examination is: We see a complicated network of similarities overlapping and crisscrossing, sometimes overall similarities, sometimes similarities of detail.

> I can think of no better expression to characterize these similarities than "family resemblances"; for the various resemblances between members of a family: build, features, colour of eyes, gait, temperament, etc., etc. overlap and criss-cross in the same way.—and I shall say: "games" form a family. (Wittgenstein, 1953, 67)

This concept is central to Wittgenstein's overall attack on essentialism, reductionism, and dualisms. Essences are replaced by family resemblances, reductionism tempts us to evade complexity, and dualisms disappear as we shift perspectives.

Thus, in a Wittgensteinian therapeutics, the search for definition of trauma, of pathology, of health, as well as of concepts specific to the particular theory, would yield to a patient form of *looking*, or as we might add, of listening. We will find ourselves wondering, musing, and watching for our own confusions and preconceptions. Maybe a term like *respect* has a positive ethical meaning for me, but a sense of terror for my patient, in whose family the term carried a threat of violence. There may be family resemblance between these meanings, but the difference of the language-games to which they belong requires attention. Otherwise we risk misunderstanding and even injury.

Confusions and misunderstandings generally result when the terms used in one language-game are taken to have the same meaning in a different one. We could say that most of Wittgenstein's philosophical work after 1930 concerned the clearing of such confusions. He criticized Freudian psychoanalysis, for example, for confusing causes and reasons. Though he respected the clinical work of psychoanalysis, he found Freud incoherent—talking nonsense—when he treated physical causes and forces as motives or reasons. Causes were irreducibly plural and joined only by family resemblance: billiard balls colliding, mechanisms like clocks and engines, human emotional reactions, and linguistic propositions ("the stock market rose because the government said . . .") are all at times called causes. Aristotle would have called these efficient causes,* in contrast to final causes like motives and reasons, for the sake of which we may act. Wittgenstein—rightly or wrongly—thought Freud was just confused, but such confusions risked reducing personal motives like desire to mechanical causes like tension reduction.

RESOURCES FOR CLINICIANS

Besides the big ideas outlined above—meaning as use, language-games, and family resemblances—Wittgenstein's thinking offers us clinicians important conceptual tools, both critical and constructive. These include both his critique of the notion of private language and his resistance to scientific reductionisms—including his appreciative critique of Freud and of the behaviorists. On the constructive side, he valued context and

---

* Aristotle distinguished four causes: formal, material, efficient, and final. His efficient cause most resembles the way we use the word *cause* today: something that happened in the past to force what we see in the present to occur. We may ask, what caused the current economic meltdown, or global warming? Final causes, on the contrary, resemble purposes, reasons, or as philosophers say, "ends." Here the future-oriented question is, for the sake of what does someone act?

complexity, and, like the phenomenologists we are also considering, he taught us to look differently at what is before our eyes. Let us begin with his famous private-language argument.

Though, to my knowledge, Wittgenstein never mentioned Descartes in this regard, and in fact rarely ever, it is easy to see his private-language argument as his challenge to the entire project of modern philosophy, with its dualisms of mind and body, inner and outer, subjectivity and objectivity, as well as its unrecognized assumptions about a representational theory of mind and a self-enclosed notion of experience and language. We are tempted, Wittgenstein thought, to imagine a language such that "the words of this language are to refer to what can be known only to the speaker; to his immediate, private, sensations. So another cannot understand the language" (Wittgenstein, 1953, 243). Not a code—which would in principle be decipherable—this language is by definition known only to one person. This, I think, is his version of the Cartesian mind, in which words refer to the "immediate private sensations" (Wittgenstein, 1953, 243) of the speaker, and he spent more than 20 pages attacking it.

The first problem with the fantasy of a private language is that without community context, there is no way to find out the meanings of the words. How, for example, do I know that you have pain? It is your pain, after all, and you must have learned a connection between sensations and their expressions. Later we learn the language-game of dissembling (Wittgenstein, 1953, 249). It is true that I cannot know for sure whether you are truly in pain, but your pain-language, even if spoken to yourself, originates only in a social context:

> How do words refer to sensations?—There doesn't seem to be any problem here; don't we talk about sensations every day, and give them names? But how is the connexion between the name and the thing named set up? This question is the same as: how does the human being learn the meaning of the names of sensations?—of the word "pain" for example. Here is one possibility: words are connected with the primitive, the natural, expressions of the sensation and used in their place. A child has hurt himself and he cries; and then adults talk to him and teach him exclamations and later, sentences. They teach the child new pain-behavior. (Wittgenstein, 1953, 224)

Even the most solitary and personal experience takes shape, we might say (Orange, 1995; Stolorow et al., 1987), in an intersubjective field or system. It makes no sense to consider experience, or language, as fully self-enclosed. In Wittgenstein's words,

Why can't my right hand give my left hand money?—My right hand can put it into my left hand. My right hand can write a deed of gift and my left hand a receipt. But the further practical consequences would not be those of a gift. When the left hand has taken the money from the right, etc. we shall ask: "well, and what of it?" And the same could be asked if a person had given himself a private definition of a word; I mean, if he has said the word to himself and at the same time has directed his attention to a sensation. (Wittgenstein, 1953, 268)

And again,

Why can't a dog simulate pain? Is he too honest? Could one teach a dog to simulate pain? Perhaps it is possible to teach him to howl on particular occasions as if he were in pain, even when he is not. But the surroundings which are necessary for this behaviour to be real simulation are missing. (Wittgenstein, 1953, 250)

Here we can see why Wittgenstein sometimes seems to be a pragmatist. If I can *do* nothing with what I seem to have "inside," then these words have no meaning. To him it was literally nonsense to think of a self-enclosed mind or private language.

Like the phenomenologists, Wittgenstein thought we tended to confuse the use of "I" as object (the container of mental representations) with "I" as subject. In the words of Hans Sluga (Sluga & Stern, 1996), Wittgenstein maintained "an enduring hostility to the idea of an individuated, substantive self" (p. 321). The subject I is instead a limit of the world, not an item within it.* Just as the physical eye cannot exist within its own visual field, but precisely limits this field, the subjective I is not an existing thing, an object. We can see that Wittgenstein's particular brand of anti-Cartesianism results from his objection to objectivism: He needed to deny subjectivity an objective existence in the world in order to save it *as subjectivity*:

Now the idea that the real I lives in my body is connected with the peculiar grammar of the word "I," and the misunderstandings this grammar is liable to give rise to. There are two different cases in the use of the word "I" (or "my") which I might call "the uses as object" and "the uses as subject." Examples of the first kind of use are these: "My arm is broken," "I have grown six inches," "I

---

* George Atwood and I discussed this idea for several years in a psychobiographical spirit. In Atwood's words, "his father designed his life and identity for him, as an engineer, and he fell into a project of fulfilling that design, until philosophy found him in his critique of objectivism in regards to the 'I,' . . . the essence of his critique of language use that turns nouns into substantives, he was using philosophical reflection to achieve what his brothers turned to suicide for: to differentiate and disentangle themselves from an epistemological monster" (personal communication, October 5, 2008).

have a bump on my forehead," "the wind blows my hair about."
Examples of the second kind are: "I see so-and-so," "I hear so-
and-so," "I try to lift my arm," "I think it will rain," "I have tooth-
ache." (Wittgenstein, 1969, pp. 66–67)

This early 1930s excerpt from what is informally referred to as the Blue
Book, precedes Wittgenstein's full development of the concept of language-games, but we can see already that the objectifying language,
both of everyday life and of scientific psychology, tends to obscure the
subjective "I." He often said that "I" and "L. W." are not the same.*

The self-enclosed subject, actually in his view an object or item, disappears as well from this story:

> Think of a picture of a landscape, an imaginary landscape with a
> house in it.—Someone asks "Whose house is that?"—The answer,
> by the way, might be "It belongs to the farmer who is sitting on
> the bench in front of it". But then he cannot for example enter his
> house. (Wittgenstein, 1953, 398)
>
> One might also say: surely the owner of the visual room would
> have to be the same kind of thing as it is: but he is not to be found
> in it, and there is no outside. (Wittgenstein, 1953, 399)†

So subjectivity is neither interiority nor exteriority, but life in the world.
For us clinicians, the shift away from interiority to living and speaking within what Wittgenstein referred to as "forms of life" is momen-
tous. Whatever our inborn capacities or temperamental propensities,
we develop a particular life only in complex relational contexts and are
never reducible to anything simple or interior. Concepts of pathology,
considered as an individual's property, give way to those of suffering,
intersubjectively generated, maintained, and possibly transformed.
Shame, no matter how isolating it feels, reappears as intrinsically social
experience, usually resulting from humiliation and contemptuous,
demeaning treatment (Orange, 2008c).

Also, a shift occurs from dualism to a philosophy of experience and
expression. Wittgenstein (or his interlocutor) asks:

> Is it the *body* that feels pain?—How is it to be decided? What makes
> it plausible to say that is *not* the body?—Well, something like this:

---

* Hans Sluga offers a caution: "It is easy to misread these anti-Cartesian arguments as sup-
porting behaviorist conclusions. We are likely to succumb to such a misreading when we
fail to notice that Wittgenstein's argument is really directed against assumptions that
the mentalist and the behaviorist share, that is, the assumptions that the subject must be
conceived as an object and that any meaningful noun or pronoun in our language must
be a name or description of an object" (Sluga, 1996b, p. 342).
† When I titled my article, "There Is No Outside," I was not conscious of quoting
Wittgenstein, but must have studied this section before that time (Orange, 2002).

if someone has a pain in his hand, then the hand does not say so (unless it writes it) and one does not comfort the hand, but the sufferer: one looks into his face. (Wittgenstein, 1953, 286)

Even less, we might imagine, could Wittgenstein think that the brain feels the pain in my hand; instead, I feel it and you see it in my face. Here is another example: "We do not see facial contortions and *make the inference* that he is feeling joy, grief, boredom. We describe a face immediately as sad, radiant, bored, even when we are unable to give any other descriptions of the features" (Wittgenstein, 1953, 570; 1980). We will find that Merleau-Ponty also argued, apparently without awareness of Wittgenstein's views, that emotion and feeling are immediately embodied and require no inference to what may be "in the mind."*

In a similar vein, Wittgenstein opposed all forms of reductionism. Though he maintained a lifelong engineering sensibility—always ready to repair something in the homes he visited or in the hospitals where he worked during the war—he shared the phenomenologists', and Dilthey's (Dilthey, 1883/1988), aversion to the worship of science. He undermined this worship, which often took the form of an insistence that only the methods of science could yield truth,† by claiming philosophical importance—much as the phenomenologists have done—for our everyday experience and ways of talking. He thought philosophers had turned off the road into insoluble problems by failing to notice what was right before their eyes.‡

Freud was a prime example. Much as Wittgenstein admired Freud (Bouveresse, 1995), he also saw him as promulgating a "charming" mythology under the guise of science. As a result, Wittgenstein thought Freud, as we have seen, had reductionistically confused reasons with causes. Causes, the kinds of dynamic and economic (quantities of "psychic energy," for example) factors to which Freudian and Kleinian instinct theories attribute our "mental" life, are pushes and pulls, fully deterministic. Reasons, the sorts of accounts we give in conversation, have value for phenomenologists and for Wittgenstein, but were disparaged by Freud as

---

* Dan Zahavi (2005) provides the parallel in Merleau-Ponty: "We must reject the prejudice which makes 'inner realities' out of love, hate or anger, leaving them accessible to one single witness: the person who feels them. Anger, shame, hate and love are not psychic facts hidden at the bottom of another's consciousness: they are types of behavior or styles of conduct which are visible from the outside. They exist *on* this face or *in* those gestures, not hidden behind them" (pp. 52–53).

† For an entertaining account of this dispute, as it took form in a debate with logical empiricist Karl Popper, see Edmonds and Eidinow (2001).

‡ Philosophy, he said, consisted in placing warnings, or assembling reminders (Wittgenstein, 1953, 127) at the crossroads where people might be tempted to turn off into misunderstanding.

defenses like denial and rationalization. What Freud failed to see, from this point of view, is that first-person experience could never be of causes, but only of reasons. Causes, whether instinctual or neurobiological or neurochemical, belong to a completely different language-game from that of meanings, reasons, and understanding. Wanting to have it both ways, Freud confused the two language-games, in which words have meanings proper to their use in each discourse.

Indeed, Wittgenstein generally resisted viewing psychology as science. "Seeing, hearing, thinking, feeling, willing," he said, "are not the subject of psychology *in the same sense as* that in which the movements of bodies, the phenomena of electricity etc., are the subject of physics" (Wittgenstein, 1953, 571). And further,

> Psychological concepts are just everyday concepts. They are not concepts newly fashioned by science for its own purpose, as are the concepts of physics and chemistry. Psychological concepts are related to those of the exact sciences as the concepts of the science of medicine are to those of old women who spend their time nursing the sick. (Wittgenstein, 1953, 62; 1980)

Replacing everyday concepts with technical shoptalk not only elevates the "scientific" jargon-speaker above the other person, but tempts us to think we know more than we do. We are misled into thinking that concepts from different language-games are interchangeable.

Another temptation in some contemporary psychoanalytic circles appears in the easy use of concepts of "mentalization" (Fonagy, 2002) without asking what such usage presumes. By mentalization, theorists mean inferring the mental states of another person. One preconception unexamined in this language-game is a representational concept of mind as a container of ideas or pictures, the very center of Wittgenstein's early work but which he spent all his later years combating. In the transitional years between his early picture-theory of ideas or representations and his later contextualism, we find this thought:

> If we scrutinize the usages which we make of such words as "thinking", "meaning," "wishing," etc., going through this process rids us of the temptation to look for a peculiar act of thinking, independent of the act of expressing our thoughts, and stowed away in some peculiar medium. We are no longer prevented by the established forms of expressions from recognizing that the experience of thinking may be just the experience of saying, or may consist of this experience plus others which accompany it. (1969, p. 43)

In other words, to notice the container notion of mind presumed by mentalization theories is to call them into question. Perhaps, just as there is

no outside, there is also no inside.* Here, to help us resist the representationalist temptation, is another Wittgenstein thought-experiment:

> Suppose everyone had a box with something in it: we call it a
> "beetle." No one can look into anyone else's box, and everyone
> says he knows what a beetle is only by looking at *his* beetle.—Here
> it would be quite possible for everyone to have something differ-
> ent in his box. One might even imagine such a thing constantly
> changing.—But suppose the word "beetle" had a use in these peo-
> ple's language?—If so it would not be used as the name of a thing.
> The thing in the box has no place in the language-game at all; not
> even as a *something*: for the box might even be empty. (1953, 293)
>
> If you say he sees a private picture before him, which he is
> describing, you have still made an assumption about what he
> has before him. And that means that you can describe it or do
> describe it more closely. If you admit that you haven't any notion
> what kind of thing it might be that he has before him—then what
> leads you into saying, in spite of that, that he has something
> before him? (1953, 294)

Such questions lead us to surmise that we do not *describe* the contents
of our minds to others, or try to guess at theirs, even through empathy,
but rather that we *express* ourselves. "I'm in pain," is another way of
saying "Ouch!" and replaces the infant's crying.

Similarly, as we have noted, though Wittgenstein admired psychoanalysis as a therapeutic process, he had no use for its theory, especially for its
postulated unconscious (Bouveresse, 1995). "Nothing is hidden," he proclaimed (Wittgenstein, 1953, 435) in a challenge both to representationalism
(Shotter, 2008) and to the Freudian unconscious. "Philosophy," he thought,
"simply puts everything before us, and neither explains nor deduces
anything.—Since everything lies open to view there is nothing to explain.
For what is hidden, for example, is of no interest to us" (Wittgenstein, 1953,
126). Instead of searching for hidden meanings and deep unconscious
motivations, he seemed to suggest, we just needed to look at our common
everyday experience from different points of view. "The aspects of things
that are most important for us are hidden because of their simplicity and
familiarity. (One is unable to notice something—because it is always before
one's eyes)" (Wittgenstein, 1953, 129).

So, for example, the patient who tells me he is depressed or confused or terrified does not need a deep "interpretation" of unconscious

---

* "We [gestalt therapists] speak of experience as emergent from the boundary of contact
between self and environment . . . experience is not private, not instinct driven, but is
emergent of the intersubjective field (or as I prefer, is context-emergent)" (L. Jacobs, personal communication, December 2, 2008).

contents or goings-on. Instead, on the assumption that what needs to be understood is right before our eyes, we engage in a conversation about what is happening, or has happened, to press him down. What kinds of mixed messages from family, culture, and so on, are confusing him? What are the sources of terror in his world? Like the phenomenologists who refer us "back to the things themselves!" Wittgenstein engages us in a dialogical effort to *notice* aspects of things—including our patients' suffering, that we had not seen because they were always before our eyes. So my depressed patient begins to tell stories that he had always "known" but never connected. Memories return, not from a reified unconscious, but from the background* contexts of our lives. Even memories and understanding dissociated by traumatic shock may be only out of view and capable of returning within therapeutic conversations. Even around a family table, one may hear "Do you remember . . .? and begin to find new ways of "seeing as" (Genova, 1995). When such "seeing as" occurs in a clinical context, we are on our way to "making sense together" (Orange, 1995).

A WITTGENSTEINIAN CLINICAL SENSIBILITY

In my view, a psychotherapeutic phenomenologist—a clinician trying to work closely and patiently with our patients' suffering—can find in Wittgenstein's therapeutic philosophy several conceptual supports.

1. A warning flag goes up whenever we are tempted to pin objectifying labels onto our patients, whether they come from diagnostic categories, or from our theories. We have probably succumbed to a tendency to essentialist reductionisms that misses the complexity of the family resemblance. We may then take comfort in a knowing "that's it!" Alternatively, we may have missed our own shift into language-games of scientific justification, games that trap us with our patients in fly-bottles (Wittgenstein, 1953, 309)[†] from which we can then not help them escape. Stuck in our

---

* For a more phenomenological but very similar account of horizonal unconsciousness, see Stolorow et al. (2002).

† Hans Sluga explains: "Fly-bottles . . . are devices for catching flies. Attracted by a sweet liquid in the bottle, the fly enters it from an opening at the bottom and when it has stilled its hunger tries to leave by flying upward toward the light. But the bottle is sealed at the top and so all attempts to escape by that route must fail. Since it never occurs to the fly to retrace its path into the bottle, it will eventually perish inside" (Sluga, 1996b, p. 338).

I have written of the fly-bottle as clinical metaphor: "We must remember how trapped, frustrated, and injured is this fly in the fly-bottle. The fly had entered though trauma, emotional violence, parental pathology, and so on. Unable to see either the way in or the way

own perspective—Wittgenstein's "aspect-blindness"—we lose contact with the experience expressed in ordinary language and gesture.

2. Wittgenstein, like the phenomenologists, engages us in constant attention to the preconceptions we bring to our work—especially to the assumption that because two people use the same word, or one person uses the same word at different times, the meaning remains constant. A gentle curiosity about words then becomes an opportunity for subtle challenges to the assumptions of both people, including emotional assumptions that one is bad, defective, outside the human community, and without hope or possibility. What Buber called dialogic inclusion becomes possible.

3. Attentiveness to difference, in language-games and in forms of life, can make us less inclined to argue about reality with our patients. My intersubjective-systems collaborators and I (Stolorow et al., 2002) have suggested that not arguing about reality can create space for acceptance and discovery, and undo the old psychoanalytic view of the therapist as the expert-authority. Though comparison of differing viewpoints may advance understanding, the treatment of our opinions and theories as points of view, unavoidably limited by our visual field, can keep us fallibilistic and prepared to learn from our patients. Especially with psychotic patients, but also with others, we prepare ourselves to learn the language-world of the other.

4. To replace all authoritarian approaches—whether Freudian interpretations, Kleinian innate aggression theories, or any theoretically based "techniques"—we can consider the possibility that *cure*, if this is the right word, might consist in shifts in ways of seeing emergent within a dialogic relationship. It takes a gestalt shift, not possible for either interlocutor alone, to see a way out of the fly-bottle. Acceptance of the complexity of

---

out, the fly repeatedly collides with the limits. Then it is often blamed for causing its own troubles, accused of projecting and of identifying with its own projections, as if the fly-bottle were not formed and maintained relationally. And we analysts must not imagine that we will be exempt from feeling what it is like in the patient's emotional world. No mechanism like projective identification is necessary to explain this" (Orange, 2008b, p. 190).

We analysts need only, through dialogue and attunement, to meet enough of the patient's emotional world to see/feel/experience/interpret this world more or less as he or she does. Otherwise, "there are problems I never get anywhere near, which do not lie in my path or are not part of my world (*nicht in meiner Linie oder in meiner Welt liegen*)" (Rhees, 1984, p. 9e; see also Orange, 2008b).

our language-games may undo dualisms, reductionisms, and temptations to search for simplified essences.

5. We might consider our clinical work as an ethical task,* the search for a decent human life for our suffering patients, as well as for ourselves as fellow sufferers. Wittgenstein, admittedly influenced by Tolstoy and Schopenhauer, saw his refusal of the reified individual mind as an ethical position. We know that he found himself deeply changed by his reading and absorption of Tolstoy's *Gospel in Brief* (Monk, 1990; Tolstoy, 1896/2008), but we might also imagine him reading Schopenhauer (1819/1969):

> If that veil of Maya, the *principium individuationis*, is lifted from the eyes of a man to such an extent that he no longer makes the egoistical distinction between himself and the person of others, but takes as much interest in the suffering of other individuals as in his own, and thus is not only benevolent and charitable in the highest degree, but even ready to sacrifice his individuality whenever several others can be saved thereby, then it follows automatically that such a man, recognizing in all beings his own true and innermost self, must also regard the endless sufferings of all lives as his own, and thus take upon himself the pain of the whole world. (vol. 1, pp. 378–379)†

As early as 1916, Wittgenstein mused: "The thinking subject is surely mere illusion. But the willing subject exists . . . the bearer of ethics" (Wittgenstein, 1979, p. 80). Though he might later have spoken differently, clearly his critique of individualized selfhood, from the war years on, had an ethical point. The purpose of the *Tractatus*, his great work of logic, was ethical. It pointed to what could not be said, only shown.

6. Finally, Wittgenstein conceived philosophy itself as a kind of therapy, including a conception of cure. He thought the resolution of philosophical problems, like that of personal difficulties, meant seeing them from points of view clear enough that they would disappear: "The real discovery is the one that makes me capable of stopping doing philosophy when I want to.—The one that gives philosophy peace so that it is no longer tormented by questions which bring *itself* into question" (1953, 133).

---

* A more obviously central concern for Emmanuel Levinas, as we will see.
† My awareness of this passage comes from Hans Sluga (Sluga, 1996a); see also Orange (2006).

To sum up, reading Wittgenstein can be a "spiritual discipline" for clinicians. Technical philosophical vocabulary is almost entirely absent; instead, he challenged us to look differently at what is right before our eyes. He warned us not to presume we know just because we use the same words. Matters are never so one-sided as they seem, but neither are they technical, scientific or unconscious. Nothing is hidden; just look!

FOR FURTHER READING

The easiest way to get into Wittgenstein may be through the superb biography *Ludwig Wittgenstein: The Duty of Genius* (Monk, 1990). For those who want help digging into the *Investigations*, I recommend *Routledge Philosophy Guidebook to Wittgenstein and the Philosophical Investigations* (McGinn, 1997).

4

MAURICE MERLEAU-PONTY
Embodied Intersubjectivity

The real is a closely woven fabric.

—Merleau-Ponty

Man is but a network of relationships, and these alone matter to him.

—Saint-Exupery, quoted in Merleau-Ponty

Like every French philosopher, Merleau-Ponty lived in the shadow of Descartes, probably on the very streets the father of modern philosophy had walked. Inspired by Husserl's phenomenology, he recast Cartesian mind-body dualism into a phenomenology of embodied experience. The no-longer-isolated mind he found woven into the world.

LIFE AND WORK

Of the philosophers we are studying, Maurice Merleau-Ponty had the least public life and rarely spoke of himself. Here is what we do know. He was born in Rochefort-sur-Mer, France, in 1908 and died in Paris in 1961 of a heart attack at the age of 53. After his father died in 1913, he lived with his mother and sister in Paris. Almost all that we know of his life before academia comes from an enigmatic remark made to his longtime friend Jean-Paul Sartre that he "had never recovered from an incomparable childhood . . . a private world of happiness from which only age drives us" (Sartre, 1964/1975).* Apart from infantry service before the fall of France in the Second World War, and resistance work during the occupation, his career was entirely academic. Studies at the École Normale Supérieure yielded as dissertations *The Structure of Behavior* (1942) and *The Phenomenology of Perception* (1945), generally considered his magnum opus. After teaching philosophy in secondary schools, Merleau-Ponty accepted the chair of child psychology at the Sorbonne in 1949, and in 1952, the prestigious chair in philosophy at the Collège de France, where he taught until his early death.

But this colorless story hides a great deal. The quiet philosopher was involved all his adult life in a relentless though respectful challenge to his whole philosophical tradition. In a spirit and style of hermeneutic generosity, he tended to present other philosophers in the best possible light and then show why it was still necessary to think differently. Similarly, he confronted the wildly popular behaviorist psychology of his time and struggled both with and against Sartre not only over Marxist theory and politics but also over what he saw as Sartre's dualism of the in-itself and for-itself. In the postwar period he was an engaged public intellectual, collaborating with Sartre to publish *Les Temps Modernes*. Like most Frenchmen, he was born both Catholic and Cartesian, but unlike many, he distanced himself early from both allegiances.

Two crucial influences—his early studies of gestalt psychology[†] and later of Husserl's phenomenology—equipped him to challenge what he called Cartesian "intellectualism." This view includes the rationalism of the modern tradition—today's "cognitivism"[‡]—as well as the empiricism and reductionism of the behaviorists. By the time he became well known in the 1940s, he was impressed by Marxism[§] and convinced that philosophy must be a life of "engagement." His complicated friendship with Jean-Paul Sartre both grew and foundered on Marxism. The Korean War convinced him, however, that the Soviet system was, in the

---

* The *Phenomenology of Perception*'s chapter on the human world begins with these loss-haunted words: "The first twenty-five years of my life (until 1933) were a prolonged childhood, destined to be followed by a painful break leading eventually to independence. If I take myself back to those years as I actually lived them and as I carry them within me, my happiness at that time cannot be explained in terms of the sheltered atmosphere of the parental home; the world itself was more beautiful, things were more fascinating" (Merleau-Ponty, 1945/2002, p. 403).

† He read especially the Berlin school: Max Wertheimer, Kurt Koffka, and Wolfgang Koehler.

‡ We can recognize this tradition in cognitive behaviorism's view that misguided ideas are the source of psychopathology.

§ "He was not a Marxist. It wasn't the idea which he rejected, but the fact that it was a dogma. . . . He reproached this intellectualism of objectivity, as he did classical rationalism, for looking the world in the face, and for forgetting that it envelops us" (Sartre, 1975, p. 237).

end, an imperialism that he could no longer support (Merleau-Ponty, 1955/1973; Sartre, 1976/1977), so he distanced himself from Sartre and withdrew to a life of teaching and writing. (See Moran, 2000, for a few more details.)

His most important contribution, by many accounts, was "a new concept of perception and its embodied relation to the world" (Carman & Hansen, 2005). Merleau-Ponty, in his last unpublished writings—interrupted by his sudden death—saw his own early work as overly dualistic and consciousness oriented. He thus, as we shall see, attempted a new philosophy of "the flesh," of the becoming visible of the invisible (Merleau-Ponty, 1968).

READING MERLEAU-PONTY

Merleau-Ponty wrote his best known work, *The Phenomenology of Perception*,* during the war and before his teaching career. This work can be difficult for many readers. Sentences can take ten lines, and paragraphs can run three pages. As commentators like Lefort and Carman have noted (Carman, 2008; Carman & Hansen, 2005), his respectful account of others' scientific work and ideas—Carman calls this his "nonadversarial dialectical strategy" (p. 25)—makes it difficult at times to discern his own views.

His posthumously published work, *The Visible and the Invisible* (Merleau-Ponty, 1964/1968), is original and opaque to most readers. I suspect that his wrenching himself away from his own lingering philosophy of consciousness (i.e., Cartesianism) inclined him both to create unfamiliar forms of expression like "flesh" and "chiasm," and also to engage in convoluted sentences, thereby creating an even greater challenge for his readers.

His lectures, however, provide easier access to his important ideas. Here (Merleau-Ponty, 1948/2004) he kept the audience in mind and used evocative metaphor to convey his main ideas. The generalized other becomes his neighbor Paul, and thinking becomes more obviously a conversation.

But let us look more closely, to see what Merleau-Ponty's work has to offer psychotherapists and psychoanalysts. Though his language and concerns may seem abstract and at times experience-distant, his philosophy of body-in-the-world can transform our clinical thinking.

---

* Merleau-Ponty's magnum opus first appeared in English in 1962. It was rereleased in 2002 in a much more readable typeface that necessitated new page numbering. I cite the 2002 edition because it is more accessible to contemporary readers.

PERCEPTION AND EMBODIMENT

Merleau-Ponty's philosophy of embodied perception includes four major claims: (a) that holism explains behavior better than dualism does; (b) that perception, like behavior, has a gestalt-like character; (c) that embodiment can become psychology's central concept; and (d) that inner and outer cannot be distinguished.

Against every kind of dualism*—mind-body, inside-outside, subject-object—Merleau-Ponty insisted on holism. Influenced especially by his studies of gestalt psychology, he began with the study of behavior and perception. Completely convinced that neither behaviors nor perceptual wholes could ever be reduced to their component parts, he anticipated what today we would call systems, complexity, and chaos theories. He would surely have agreed with the famous dictum of physicist Philip Anderson (1972) that *more is different* and with the gestalt maxim that the whole is more (or strictly speaking, different) than the sum of its parts. Behavior, Merleau-Ponty argued against the classical behaviorists, can only be understood holistically, not in terms of isolated instances of stimulus and response (as behaviorists had tried to do). A child who touches a hot stove does not learn an isolated response, but a whole gestalt of responsiveness. "It is not the violent reaction which follows a painful experience that is established in a child's behavior, but rather reactions of protection" (Merleau-Ponty, 1942/1963, pp. 98–99). It is the larger meaning of the situated experience which establishes itself in the child's life and obviates the dualisms.†

After his early holistic studies of behavior, Merleau-Ponty traveled to Louvain to study the manuscripts of Edmund Husserl. From Husserl's phenomenology he learned to be a perpetual beginner in philosophy. For Husserl this "reduction," much like Descartes' methodical doubt, meant stripping away all preconceptions and attempting to find a pure subjectivity that could then constitute objective things. For Merleau-Ponty, on the contrary, the perpetual beginning was, as for Heidegger (1927/1962), always already situated in a world. In contrast to Descartes' focus on mind—precisely defined as that which is not body—Merleau-Ponty studied the situated body-subject and embodied intersubjectivity.

---

* In the words of M. C. Dillon (1997), "It is a matter of chance . . . whether future historians attribute to Merleau-Ponty or to some currently unknown philosophical clone writing in another idiom the unplugging of the flow of Western thought. The plug is dualism. It has to come out. Merleau-Ponty shows us how" (p. xviii).

† Merleau-Ponty's solution to dualism was not a Hegelian synthesis of opposites. Instead he rethought the polarization in question and struggled for concepts that make the original duality unnecessary.

The Gestalt influences, we might say, moderated or even transformed what he learned of phenomenology from Husserl.

The Phenomenology of Perception consists of elaborate studies of perceptual processes that, he insisted, could never be extricated from their situatedness.* Nor could they be rightly described either as mental or physical processes. The gestalt, the thing perceived, is not outside my world; it exists for the perceiving subject. The printer on my desk is not, as perceived, an object in a world outside; it exists for me, for my purposes, and for the use of anyone else who uses it. It has a rudimentary reality apart from me, but it exists as a set of possibilities for human purposes. Moreover, the gestalt psychologists, as appropriated by Merleau-Ponty, believed that embodied perception structures itself around expectations of wholeness, of completeness, and a sense of rightness or equilibrium. "To pay attention," for example, "is not merely to elucidate pre-existing data, it is to bring about a new articulation of them by taking them as figures. They are preformed only as horizons, they constitute in reality new regions in the total world" (Merleau-Ponty, 1945/2002, p. 35). Experience is never atomistic, cobbled together from bits of sense data, but rather is inescapably holistic.

It is a short step from a gestalt view of behavior and a holistic concept of perception to a full philosophy of embodiment. We are our bodies (Merleau-Ponty, 1945/2002, p. xii). As Taylor Carman (2008, p. 6) puts it, "Merleau-Ponty's central philosophical idea is that perception is a bodily phenomenon, not a mental event occurring at the end of a chain of physical causes and events, as Descartes supposed." A relentless descriptive study of lived experience, pursued in a phenomenological sprit, undoes dualism. For Merleau-Ponty—unlike the Heidegger of *Being and Time* (1927/1962), for whom embodiment was a footnote or less in philosophy—embodied being was the key to understanding our being-in-the-world.† Heidegger's being-in-the-world (*In-der-Welt-sein*) and Merleau-Ponty's *être au monde* meant that we were "always already" (Heidegger's expression) situated and never unrelated to our context. For Merleau-Ponty, however, the emphasis was on embodied perception and the way it gives us access to the world in which we always already live. Ever interested in experimental psychology, he wanted to know

---

* Merleau-Ponty owed an enormous and largely unacknowledged debt to Heidegger's being-in-the-world. For reasons he did not, to my knowledge, explain, he more easily gave credit to Edmund Husserl's influence on him, even though he often reshaped Husserl's ideas in a Heideggerian direction.

† I thank both Roger Frie and Robert Stolorow for reminding me that in the *Zollikoner Seminare* (Heidegger & Boss, 2001), Heidegger engaged embodiment directly as a mode of being-in-the-world.

how proprioception (the sense of one's own body) works and what various perceptual disorders could tell us about the nature of perception.

Opposed to every form of dualism, Merleau-Ponty concluded that inner and outer could not be adequately distinguished. Like Wittgenstein (1953), he argued that there is no private inner being, but only the embodied and perceiving being in the world. Nor is the world fully outside, but only accessible to perception. Not that, as the poststructuralists would later hold, there is nothing to know. For Merleau-Ponty, "the real has to be described, not constructed or formed" (1945/2002, p. xi). His version of phenomenology—more everyday and familiar than Husserl's and also less esoteric than Heidegger's—described all experience from the viewpoint of embodied perception.

COGNITIVE NEUROSCIENCE WITHOUT REDUCTIONISM

Merleau-Ponty's lifelong propensity to address psychological research seriously would probably have led him to intensive discussions of today's cognitive neuroscience (Clark, 2001; Damasio, 1994, 1999, 2003; LeDoux, 1996;). He always thought phenomenology and the empirical sciences shared a common ground—the world of perception. Evocatively he claimed that

> the sun "rises" for the scientist in the same way as it does for the uneducated person, and our scientific representations of the solar system remain matters of hearsay, like lunar landscapes, and we never believe in them in the sense in which we believe in the sunrise. (1945/2002, p. 401)

He would have studied the purposes of the neuroscientists, their technological methods, their findings, and the conclusions they draw from their work. Of particular interest to him might have been the ideas of Antonio Damasio (1994), opponent of bifurcation. Damasio claims, persuasively, that a neurobiology of emotion can best help us to understand consciousness. Descartes' error, encapsulated in the *cogito* "I think therefore I am," was to imagine, in Gilbert Ryle's (1959) famous and scornful words, a "ghost in the machine." For Damasio and for most cognitive neuroscientists, there is no ghost, only an utterly fascinating machine that misleads us into thinking/feeling that we have souls.

Merleau-Ponty, as Hubert Dreyfus (2005) explains, would have believed that a nonreductionist, holistic phenomenology would take seriously everything the cognitive neuroscientists are learning and theorizing about our brains. He would have agreed wholeheartedly with the rejection of representationalism by cognitive scientists like Andy

Clark (2001), Shaun Gallagher (2005), and David Chalmers (2002) and with their search for nonreductionist explanations of consciousness. Representational theories of mind, like correspondence theories of truth, envision mind as a container of images or of verbal copies of things. The problem of representation arises because there is no way to compare inner and outer. Merleau-Ponty thought there must be something wrong with representation itself as a view of how we are in the world. But he would have seen Damasio, and especially LeDoux, as interested primarily in the *individual* mind/brain. Merleau-Ponty, on the contrary, insisted that we can understand ourselves only as born into and always already woven into a social world. "My body," he wrote, "is a movement towards the world, and the world my body's point of support" (1945/2002, p. 408).*

Not that a phenomenologist need be hostile to science. Instead, in Merleau-Ponty's (1948/2004) words,

> the question is whether science does, or even could, present us with a picture of the world which is complete, self-sufficient and somehow closed in upon itself, such that there could no longer be any meaningful questions outside this picture. It is not a matter of denying or limiting the extent of scientific knowledge, but rather of establishing whether it is entitled to deny or rule out as illusory all forms of inquiry that do not start from measurements and comparisons and, by connecting particular causes with particular consequences, end up laws such as those of classical physics. (p. 43)

Our temptation is "to hold science and knowledge in such high esteem that all our lived experience of the world seems by contrast to be of little value" (p. 40). He believed that scientific knowledge "cannot be closed in on itself, that it is always an approximate knowledge, and that it consists in clarifying a pre-scientific world the analysis of which will never be finished" (1964a, p. 20). We phenomenologists need not reject science, but we see it as derivative from the more practical demands of worlded embodiment.

Merleau-Ponty would find subjectivity irreducible and inseparable from its material conditions. Like Thomas Nagel (1974), in his famous "What is it like to be a bat?" he might ask what it is like to feel tired. He might ask what it is like to have someone imaging your brain as they ask

---

* "Freudians have often claimed that phenomenological and relational perspectives neglect the body. Merleau-Ponty's philosophy of embodied perception and embodied intersubjectivity is a definitive refutation of this claim" (R. Stolorow, personal communication, December 9, 2008).

you questions or otherwise involve you in experiments. Merleau-Ponty, phenomenologist to the core, could never subtract out the experience, this what-is-it-like-ness, similar to Heidegger's *Befindlichkeit* (Heidegger, 1927/1962; see also Gendlin, 1979). If neuroscience produces usable information about the material conditions for the possibility of cognitive and emotional functioning, there could be important practical consequences.* But, Merleau-Ponty (1964a) would claim:

> The perceiving mind is an incarnated mind. I have tried, first of all to reestablish the roots of the mind in its body and in its world, going against doctrines which treat perception as a simple result of the action of external things on our body as well as against those which insist on the autonomy of consciousness. These philosophies commonly forget—in favor of a pure exteriority or of a pure interiority—the insertion of the mind in corporeality, the ambiguous relation which we entertain with our body and, correlatively, with perceived things. (pp. 3–4)

Or again: "The bond between the soul and the body is not a parallelism, . . . nor is it absolute opacity. . . . It is to be understood as the bond between the convex and the concave, between the solid vault and the hollow it forms" (Merleau-Ponty, 1964/1968, p. 232).

At this time, of course, the dialogues between phenomenology and cognitive neuroscience continue, and the outcomes are various and uncertain. Neuroscience, with its gee-whiz appeal, garners more press attention, but its more representationalist and reductionist forms do seem to be moderating in a humanistic direction. At the same time phenomenologists are beginning to learn from neuroscience (Gallagher & Zahavi, 2008). Perhaps long-dead phenomenologists like Merleau-Ponty deserve some credit for this.

CLINICAL IMPLICATIONS: A FIRST LOOK

How does a philosophy of embodied perception matter to our clinical work? Already I think we can pick out three important themes:

1. Both patient and therapist will inevitably describe from the viewpoint of embodied perception. Neither will have access

---

* American philosopher Charles Sanders Peirce (1839–1914) formulated his famous pragmatic maxim: "Consider what effects, which might conceivably have practical bearings, we conceive the object of our conception to have. Then the whole of our conception of those effects is the whole of our conception of the object" (1878/1992, p. 132). He illustrated with the concept of hardness, showing that the word has no more meanings than the sum of its conceivable practical effects.

to the kind of outside or abstracted knowledge that results in diagnostic categories. A young woman came to me with complex problems: obsessions, overwhelming feelings that she must harm herself immediately, and hearing voices. She found it almost impossible to trust anyone, least of all herself. I understood from the beginning that I was a frightening person, but only gradually came to see why. In about the sixth session, she confessed, "I am so afraid you will say I am a borderline." "Why would I do that?" I asked. "Because that's what the hospital social workers told my parents," she responded. "And what do you think they meant by that?" I asked. "I don't know," she said, "but I think it's something really bad, and I want to know if you think I have it, and if it's something that can get better." A phenomenologist would instead have responded to her embodied suffering in a world of misunderstanding and humiliation.

2. Details—symptoms, episodic memories, and so on—take on meaning only in the context of ongoing and embodied being in the world. This means not only that meanings evolve within contexts, both in treatment and in life, but also that there is rarely a need to argue about reality.

> Sara, a brilliant and accomplished 27-year-old with a history of religious delusions, cult involvement, and a childhood that resembled an emotional prison camp, called me one day in a panic. "You have to help me. I went to Baltimore where I stayed with five friends from college. The next-door neighbors told us about the ghosts in their house, and things being moved, and strange noises and all sorts of weird things. We all had a good time, and my friends went home, but I am completely terrified. I feel these ghosts will follow me to New York and come after me. I don't know why, but I feel it is true, and I am completely and totally scared. I can't do anything but think about it." After asking a few questions about the ghosts and about various aspects of the whole situation—questions that led nowhere—I said firmly: "Sara, I have always heard that ghosts like to stay in their own houses and don't like to travel. I believe these ghosts have no interest in you." "Really?" she asked, "Please tell me again." Without any sense of where my conviction came from, I repeated my statement in the same tone of voice. "Thank you," she said, sounding very relieved. She returned immediately to functioning well, and has not mentioned the ghosts again. (Orange, in press)

Their "reality" was probably their meaning in a life where usurpation of her sense of agency had left her feeling ever vulnerable

to "dementors" (Rowling, 1999). My response evidently reposi-
tioned her in a safer relational world.

3. Attunement to embodied presence and absence (dissociation) can provide a means of lived connection in therapy and
psychoanalysis. From the gestalt therapists' attentiveness to
emotion's body-expression, to the focusing on embodied
experience pioneered by Eugene Gendlin (1996), through
the somatically oriented reveries of Thomas Ogden (1997),
through the "unformulated experience" of Donnel Stern
(1997) and through all the forms of sensory process described
as self and mutual regulation by Beatrice Beebe and Frank
Lachmann (2001), contemporary clinical work owes a large
debt to Merleau-Ponty's phenomenology of existence incarnate. All these authors have made explicit use of Merleau-
Ponty's phenomenology.

SKILLED COPING AND SITUATED TEMPORALITY

The crucial and irreducible character of embodied subjectivity, or of
the "body-subject," is its situatedness. My situation is not just my location on a map; in my experiential world I find myself incarnated and
always participant. Within this world I must cope, in situations that
range from the most mundane, for example, adjusting to a new key-
board, to the most complex, for example, maneuvering within a complex interpersonal situation (Dreyfus, 1992). Merleau-Ponty thought
that our capacity for skilled coping—getting a maximal grip or grasp—
was the best argument against the representational theory of mind. In
Carman's (2008) words, "To perceive is not to have inner mental states,
but to know and find your way around in an environment" (p. 19).* It
involves a personal and unrepeatable style of being in the world. Skilled
coping was, for Merleau-Ponty, our incarnated existence.

But, again, how does this matter to us clinicians? It is already a truism
to practitioners of the talking therapies that context matters: developmental contexts, cultural and economic contexts, contemporaneous intersubjective contexts particularly. What I think the emphasis on skilled coping
provides, apart from its resistance to reductionist explanations, is an
emphasis on the future, especially on the immediate future.† My project

---

* Carman continues: "Our sense organs are not cameras and recording devices, and our
minds are not calculators" (p. 20).

† Lynne Jacobs (personal communication, December 15, 2008) notes that she thinks of
trauma-generating conditions as impairing the development of needed emotional skills
(see also Taylor, 1985).

may be to create the most profitable Scrabble word while preventing my opponent from doing even better. Or it may be to find a way around a traffic jam. Or it may be to manage a misunderstanding so that it will not generate long-term damage to an important relationship. All day and every day, we are engaged in skilled-coping projects. "My body appears to me as a posture with a view to a certain actual or possible task.... If I stand in front of my desk and lean on it with both hands, only my hands are accentuated and the whole of my body trails behind them like the tail of a comet" (Merleau-Ponty, 1945/2002, pp. 114–115). Conversely—and I owe awareness of this juxtaposition to Taylor Carman—"I know where my pipe is with absolute certainty, and *thereby* I know where my hand is and where my body is" (1945/2002, p. 115). This is what embodied thinking looks like. To manage in our situations, we shift from the "I think" to the "I am able to" (Merleau-Ponty, 1960/1964c, p. 88).

In our daily clinical work, suffering people come to us feeling that they cannot cope. They feel overwhelmed by trauma, sorrow, resentment, interpersonal misunderstandings, and so on. Now what would skilled coping mean in these situations? It is not a question of learning to walk, to ride a bicycle, or to say something gracious when receiving an unpleasing gift. It is more like finding oneself in a strange house that is supposed to be one's home. So I often describe the project to patients as learning to find one's way around in one's own situated emotional life, as becoming familiar with one's experiential world. This includes becoming familiar with one's embodied experience, as some body and gestalt therapies teach us. It also means, most often, discovering and integrating one's developmental/relational history, so that one can recognize the sedimented* (already constituted) meanings (Merleau-Ponty, 1945/2002, p. 150), organizing principles (Atwood & Stolorow, 1984; Stolorow et al., 1987), working models (Bowlby, 1979), or emotional convictions (Orange, 1995) that unconsciously structure our lives and relationships in ways that seem automatic. Skilled coping in the emotional life can mean developing both familiarity with these sedimentations and the means of loosening their grip on us so that we can have more sense of agency and choice.

---

* Dillon (1997) illustrates Merleau-Ponty's concept of sedimentation with dualism itself: "Sedimentation is the settling of culture into things. In our culture, the separation of the animate and the inanimate has permeated all things; it is, perhaps, the most deeply entrenched of all dualisms; it permeates our language, our thought, and the things themselves. There is no *epoche* [bracketing] capable of freeing us in one act of reflection from millennia of sediment; it is, rather, the work of a lifetime to form the *askesis* [training, striving] required to dig out from under the conceptual weight of the dualist tradition" (p. 101).

Heidegger's authenticity (*Eigentlichkeit, Jemeinigkeit*) would have seemed to Merleau-Ponty too individualistic to account for such situated experience. Likewise, Merleau-Ponty thought Sartre's absolute freedom an illusion. Instead he emphasized the limited freedom of finding our way:

> I can miss being free only if I try to bypass my natural and social situation by refusing to take it up, in the first place, instead of assuming it in order to join up with the natural and human world. Nothing determines me from outside, not because nothing acts upon me, but on the contrary, because I am from the start outside myself and open to the world. We are *true* through and through, and have with us, by the mere fact of belonging to the world, and not merely being in the world in the way that things are, all that we need to transcend ourselves. (1945/2002, pp. 529–530)

In other words, to be true or genuine is to live the relatedness that we already are, to believe in and commit oneself to a world.

In his unfinished last work, Merleau-Ponty described a "perceptual faith" that allows us "to believe that what is for us is absolutely, that a world we have succeeded in seeing as without danger is without danger . . . that our vision goes to the things themselves" (Merleau-Ponty, 1964/1968, p. 28). He explained:

> It is our experience, prior to every opinion, of inhabiting the world by our body, of inhabiting the truth by our whole selves, without there being need to choose nor even to distinguish between the assurance of seeing and the assurance of seeing the true, because in principle they are one and the same thing—faith, therefore, and not knowledge, since the world is here not separated from our hold on it, since, rather than affirmed, it is taken for granted. (p. 28)

It is this "perceptual faith" that psychological trauma destroys (Stolorow, 2007), or prevents from ever really being established. Where some patients can point to the moment of annihilation of their "sense of things," of their "innocence," others inhabit a world so precarious that they can remember no time of perceptual faith. At its best, perceptual faith is only a fragile faith—not knowledge—but it makes possible the development of capacities for coping in a world.

Even working with adolescents, I have found that a skilled-coping focus can be very helpful. We cannot change the parents, or anything about the past. But an approach that says, "Let's figure it out together, and see what's possible" can often help. This attitude embodies the recognition that the situation is difficult, painful, frustrating, and seems hopeless, but also it lives a faith and hope in the capacity of the patient.

Initially this capacity resides in the intersubjective field of parent and child, therapist/analyst and patient: Let's figure it out together. But later, the voice of the other becomes a usable resource, some would say an "integrated" aspect, of this attitude that says skilled coping is possible.

Every instance or task of skilled coping is saturated with lived temporality. My situation is always already filled with sedimented meanings—the opaque past become present—and with projects for getting this maximal grasp, the future become present. There is no atomic present, no isolated instant. The "present moment," to use Stern's (2004) felicitous phrase, is situated and inextricable. As a note loses all meaning apart from its musical context, and a word apart from its use (Wittgenstein, 1953), so must a moment remain temporally embedded in order to be a moment at all.

In addition to the sedimented though ambiguous presence of the past in every moment, Merleau-Ponty (1960/1964c) also evoked what he called "advent" (p. 68), an expression he borrowed from phenomenologist Paul Ricoeur (1955/1965). By "advent" he meant the capacity of every cultural expression to exceed itself, "to inaugurate a meaning." Merleau-Ponty thus reminds us clinicians that development may be understood not only as past-loaded, but also as forward-pointing, the "leading edge" described by Heinz Kohut (1996). Working with the leading edge within an intersubjective field allows us to notice not only the "repetitive dimensions" (Stolorow et al., 1987), but also the coming advent, both personal and cultural. Cultural expressions then become "several ways for the human body to sing the world's praises and in the last resort to live it" (Merleau-Ponty, 1945/2002, p. 218).

INTERSUBJECTIVITY AND REVERSIBILITY

The concept of intersubjectivity came into philosophy about 200 years ago in the responses to Kant's critical philosophy (Frie & Reis, 2001). Claiming that knowing requires both innate ideas and sense experience, Kant had found a path between the dogmatic rationalism of the Cartesians and the skeptical empiricism of Hume. Merleau-Ponty, however, found Kant himself too full of "intellectualism," too full of "consciousness," and in need of a world:

> The Kantian subject posits a world, but in order to be able to assert a truth, the actual subject must in the first place have a world or be in the world, that is, sustain round about it a system of meanings whose reciprocities, relationships and involvements do not require to be made explicit in order to be exploited. (1945/2002, p. 149)

Merleau-Ponty situated the Kantian subject, but once situated in a world, this subject largely disappears. There is no mind lurking behind the body, rather body is mind incarnate in the world.

For Merleau-Ponty then, there is no perception and no world without intersubjectivity (or "communion"); the social world is indispensable to embodiment. There is no philosophical "problem of other minds"; instead, as Carman (2008) puts it, "Others are not a problem, but they are trouble" (p. 146). For Merleau-Ponty, "The perception of other people and the intersubjective world is problematical only for adults. The child lives in a world which he unhesitatingly believes accessible to all around him" (1945/2002, p. 413). And the child is right, Piaget (and the theorists of mentalization) notwithstanding: "The unsophisticated thinking of our earliest years remains as an indispensable acquisition underlying that of maturity, if there is to be for the adult one single intersubjective world" (1945/2002, p. 413). In other words, as body-subjects, we are involved with and in the world on a prereflective level. We live with each other in an intersubjective system completely irreducible to our consciousness of ourselves, others, or of this world. "Our own body," he said, "is in the world as the heart is in the organism" (1945/2002, p. 235).

This world is a system of intricate inhabitation, a common ground. This system forms the only basis for our communication. The other inhabits the same world with me, so that we are able to be in communication:

> In the experience of dialogue, there is constituted between the other person and myself a common ground; my thought and his are inter-woven into a single fabric, my words and those of my interlocutor are called forth by the state of the discussion, and they are inserted into a shared operation of which neither of us is the creator . . . . we are collaborators for each other in consummate reciprocity. Our perspectives merge into each other, and we co-exist through a common world. (Merleau-Ponty, 1945/2002, p. 413)

We can see here that intersubjectivity for Merleau-Ponty has a double character: As world it forms the necessary condition for the possibility of any communication at all, but it also further emerges from the conversation. (We will find Gadamer saying something quite similar, as we have already heard from Buber.)

The practical relevance of this embodied intersubjectivity is clearest when we turn to the clinician's central concern, the emotional life. Merleau-Ponty's (1948/2004) discussion of anger makes it clear that he has fully rejected an isolated-mind view of emotion:

> Imagine that I am in the presence of someone who, for one reason or another, is extremely annoyed with me. My interlocutor

gets angry and I notice that he is expressing his anger by speaking aggressively, by gesticulating and shouting. But where is this anger? People will say that it is in the mind of my interlocutor. What this means is not entirely clear. For I could not imagine the malice and cruelty which I discern in my opponent's looks separated from his gesture, speech and body. None of this takes place in some otherworldly realm, in some shrine located beyond the body of the angry man. It is really here, in this room and in this part of the room that the anger unfolds. It is in the space between him and me that it unfolds. (p. 83)

Even if we are speaking on the telephone and the rage comes through my interlocutor's voice, it is embodied and exists in the intersubjective field or space. When the situation is reversed, and I am "the angry one," the same thing holds. Merleau-Ponty continued:

When I reflect on my own anger, I do not come across any element that might be separated or, so to speak, unstuck from my own body. When I recall being angry at Paul, it does not strike me that this anger was in my mind or among my thoughts but rather, that it lay entirely between me who was doing the shouting and that odious Paul who just sat there calmly and listened with an ironic air. (p. 84)

Only later, Merleau-Ponty explained, do I think that a negative evaluation of Paul resides in me or in my mind. Where the Cartesian container-mind concept had subtracted out embodiment, experience, and intersubjectivity, subjectivity now becomes our involvement in the world. "Inside and outside are inseparable. The world is wholly inside and I am wholly outside myself" (1945/2002, p. 474). As a body-subject I am just a perspective on and in the world, a worlded and committed subjectivity. "The body is our anchorage in a world" (1945/2002, p. 167), and again, "The body is our general medium for having a world" (1945/2002, p. 169).

In his posthumously published and unfinished *The Visible and the Invisible* (1964/1968), the concept of reversibility intrigued Merleau-Ponty.* Intersubjectivity had always meant reversibility: What we touch inevitably also touches us. Now he asked: Is visibility also reversible? If I can see the other (even a tree), does this mean that the other can see me? Is the other my mirror? If so, does the mirror see me as I see it? No, he thought: The mirror reflects me, it does not see me. I see my reflection in the mirror, I do not see myself with all the proprioception and limitations (I can sense something behind my back, but cannot see my back). He

---

* I am indebted for the understandings in this paragraph to Dillon (1997).

concluded that there is a fundamental asymmentry within intersubjectivity, within the flesh that we both are. We cannot, Scottish poet Robert Burns to the contrary,* see ourselves as others see us. Shaking hands is not the same as touching one's own hand; some part of the other's experience remains inaccessible to me. Touching my other hand differs from touching the hand touching the tree. In Merleau-Ponty's words:

> Reversibility of the seeing and the visible, of the touching and the touched . . . is a reversibility always imminent and never realized in fact. My left hand is always on the verge of touching my right hand touching the things, but I never reach coincidence . . . . Likewise, I do not hear myself as I hear the others, the sonorous existence of my voice is for me as it were poorly exhibited; I have rather an echo of its articulated existence, it vibrates through my head rather than outside. *I am always on the same side of my body.* (Merleau-Ponty, 1964/1968, pp. 147–148).

We have here a double asymmetry within our common world: The other sees and feels me as I cannot possibly feel myself, and I feel myself as the other cannot possibly feel me.

HUMAN LIFE: AMBIGUOUS, INTRICATE, AND PRECARIOUS

Merleau-Ponty believed that human life was ambiguous, intricate, and precarious. By "ambiguous" he meant that most of the opposites or dualisms we set up or take for granted need a more inclusive view. The answer usually is both-and, but not in a simplistic way. We are neither body nor mind, but body-subjects. We are both alone and dependent on others at every moment. "If we are in a situation, we are surrounded and cannot be transparent to ourselves, so that our contact with ourselves is necessarily achieved only in the sphere of ambiguity" (Merleau-Ponty, 1945/2002, p. 444). This ambiguity excludes the "clear and distinct ideas" criterion of truth we have inherited from Descartes, but also Hegel's master-slave dialectic of domination and submission, as well as Sartre's reductive gaze in *La Nausée* (Sartre, 1938/1979), for example. Responding both to Hegel and to Sartre, Merleau-Ponty wrote:

> The other's gaze transforms me into an object, and mine him, only if both of us withdraw into the care of our thinking, if we both

---

* O wad some Power the giftie gie us,
  To see oursels as ithers see us!
  It wad frae mony a blunder free us,
  An' foolish notion.

make ourselves into an inhuman gaze, if each of us feels his actions to be not taken up and understood, but observed as if they were an insect's. This is what happens, for instance, when I fall under the gaze of a stranger. But even then, the objectification of each by the other's gaze is felt as unbearable only because it takes the place of possible communication. A dog's gaze directed towards me causes me no embarrassment. The refusal to communicate, however, is still a form of communication. (1945/2002, p. 420)

We see that possible communication contravenes the objectifying opposition, in which we can feel haunted by Kafka's giant cockroach (Kafka & Corngold, 1996) and Camus' stranger (Camus & Gilbert, 1946). The ambiguity, however, remains: Whose gaze is it anyway?

Such ambiguity results from the intricacy of our situated being in the world. Another word for complexity, *intricacy* expresses intertwined involvement, the impossibility of dualism, and irreducibility of our embodied experience to any simple notion of subjectivity. Ambiguity and intricacy leave our lives precarious:

> Humanity is precarious: each person can only believe what he recognizes to be true internally and, at the same time, nobody thinks or makes up his mind without already being caught up in certain relationships with others, which leads him to opt for a particular set of opinions. Everyone is alone and yet nobody can do without other people. (Merleau-Ponty, 1948/2004, p. 87)

In fact, he gave a surprising defense of Sartre's dictum that "hell is other people":

> If other people are the instruments of our torture, it is first and foremost because they are indispensable to our salvation. We are so intermingled with them that we must make what order we can out of this chaos. Sartre [in *No Exit*] put Garcin in Hell not for being a coward but for having made his wife suffer. (Merleau-Ponty, 1964b, p. 41)

So this intricate intermingling implies an ethics. Though Merleau-Ponty said little directly about ethics, his work could perhaps be described as a moral phenomenology (Levin, 1998),* one that confronts us clinicians with our daily situation: involvement with the devastation left by psychological trauma.

---

* "The trial and death of Socrates would not have remained a subject of reflection and commentary if it had only been an incident in the struggle of evil men against good men and had one not seen in it an innocent man who accepts his sentence, a just man who obeys conscience and yet refuses to reject the world and obeys the *polis*, meaning that it belongs to man to judge the law *at the risk of being judged by it*" (Merleau-Ponty, 1947/1980, p. xxxviii-xxxix).

TRAUMATIC LIVING MEMORY

Merleau-Ponty's concepts of embodied memory or sedimentation (see above) come together for me in what I have called traumatic living memory (2009, in press). By this I mean more than what is usually described as procedural memory: knowing how to ride a bicycle, or how to reach for something. I mean something like what I once called "emotional memory" (1995), referring to the enduring felt quality of a process or interaction.* This quality is usually difficult to express in denotative language and lends itself better to metaphor and to expression through the arts. Emotional memory is lived primarily bodily and constitutes the largest part of our lifeworld. It has gentle forms, like the recognition of a very particular smile, but it becomes especially salient for our work in worlds of trauma and of retraumatization.

Embodiment is more than just brain function, but rather the experience of the total situated living system. Embodiment is lived and living experience. When my patient says, "My brain tells me that it won't hurt me, but the rest of me knows that it will," the "rest of me," she goes on, is the me that feels, that knows how dangerous certain people really are, based on traumatic living memory. I respond to my patient that she knows it (whatever it is) in her whole being, in every inch of her body. This knowing memory may be more or less verbal, more or less explicit, more or less conscious.

In other words, I believe that we need to see this new dualism of implicit and explicit—along with inner and outer, intrapsychic and relational, mind and body, unconscious and conscious—as the reification of experiential qualities of our being-in-the-world. Such reifications take form—as my collaborators and I have shown in our studies of psychosis (Stolorow & Atwood, 1992; Orange, Atwood, & Stolorow, 1997; Stolorow et al., 2002)—in relational conditions that create extreme vulnerability without validation or support. In these traumatizing situations, the experiential world becomes radically divided along lines that can become rigid categories of thought. Like rape victims whose world becomes suddenly, violently, and rigidly split into the safe and the unsafe, thinkers seem to "find" their worlds divided into implicit and explicit, procedural and narrative, embodied and symbolic.†

---

* At that time I wrote: "Our history resides in our whole being" (p. 120). This view places me closer to the ideas of Gendlin (1979) and of Preston and Shumsky (2002) than to the implicit/explicit dualists.

† See our discussion (Stolorow et al., 2002) of the traumatic history of the philosopher Descartes, who gave us the original modern dualisms of mind and body, subject and object, inner and outer, reason and imagination. See also Orange (in press) on speaking the unspeakable.

Merleau-Ponty's world in its original rich and growing complexity becomes a split world, not only defensively but experientially. The danger, for example, of making a mistake or of doing something that might leave them vulnerable to criticism keeps many patients paralyzed. From unfinished dissertations and relationships never resolved in one direction or another, to the hours spent deciding which socks to wear, we live in worlds frozen by fear of crossing over to the unsafe side. Time stands still. Robert Frost's two roads that diverge create a situation of extreme danger, in which there is no opportunity to work out a life whichever choice one makes. Such clinical situations confront us every day with the challenge of finding ways to soften the absolute quality of these everyday dualisms. This experiential absoluteness, brought into question, finds little response beyond "I can't." It lies in the region of the experiential continuum that I have called "the unspeakable."

MERLEAU-PONTY AND PSYCHOANALYSIS

Merleau-Ponty engaged Freudian psychoanalysis in much the same way as he did Husserl's phenomenology and the work of the gestalt psychologists. Each, he believed, offered something indispensable to the understanding of human life, but missed the perspective of embodied intersubjectivity. The gestaltists showed how perception picks out a figure from the background in perception (Merleau-Ponty, 1945/2002, p. 78), and Husserl taught us to suspend our theories long enough to go "back to the things themselves."

Early on, Merleau-Ponty (1963) faulted Freud for an inadequate view of psychological development: It is not "the fixation of a given force on outside objects which are also given, but . . . a progressive and discontinuous structuration of behavior" (p. 177). Freud failed to understand development, Merleau-Ponty implied, because he missed the forest for the trees, the bits of behavior for the whole field of meaning.

In his later work, Merleau-Ponty sometimes took up these trees—behaviors, complexes, and so on—and reread them as modes of human being in the world. Where sexuality had been for Freud a content of the individual's conscious or unconscious mind, it became for Merleau-Ponty a mode of being, an attitude, that occurs in a world. What Freud had seen was the importance of human sexuality; Merleau-Ponty saw its importance as a crucial mode of embodied worlded existence. In the words of Askay and Farquhar (2005),

> Psychoanalysis [Merleau-Ponty's version] allowed for the expansion of the notion of sexuality so as to absorb into it the world

of existence. By doing so, the true relationship existing between sexuality and existence can be explored. The two exist as inter-woven and inseparable intentionalities. Multiple meanings result from the ambiguity of the bodily subject because its numerous parts permeate and interpenetrate one another. (p. 297)

So Merleau-Ponty, in his last years, read Freud as moving toward his own philosophy of the flesh (*le chair*). Mind (conscious or unconscious) and body are now gone. Now we have the flesh, the body-world, in which id, ego, and superego appear as modes. A more primordial incarnate consciousness replaces the Freudian unconscious. "Consciousness is now the 'soul of Heraclitus' [fire] and Being, which around it rather than in front of it is the Being of dreams, by definition hidden" (Merleau-Ponty, 1969, p. 85).

Thus, as usual for him, Merleau-Ponty credited Freud for what he had noticed, and then read him through the lens of his own existential phenomenology,* where terms that seem to be jargon retain hints of their experiential origins:

> The best . . . would perhaps be . . . to learn to read Freud the way we read a classic, that is by understanding his words and theoretical concepts, not in the lexical and common meaning, but in the meaning they acquire from within the experience which they announce and of which we have behind our backs more than a suspicion . . . perhaps we should continue calling it the unconscious†—so long as we do not forget that the word is the index of an enigma—because the term retains, like the algae or the stone that one drags up, something of the sea from which it was taken. (Merleau-Ponty, 1969, p. 86)

Though Freud considered phenomenology too focused on the psychological surface, and Merleau-Ponty gave only this grudging consent to "the unconscious," each in his own way stressed the embodied situation.

It seems to me notable, however, that some strains of contemporary psychoanalysis—especially Kohut's self psychology and intersubjective systems theory—fit Merleau-Ponty's world even better than Freud's did. Of course self psychology emerged after Merleau-Ponty's death, but the themes of coherence and fragmentation seem strongly kindred. Kohut's (1959) essay

---

* A very helpful account of Merleau-Ponty's engagement with Freud appears in Askay and Farquhar (2005).

† "The unconscious, then was not an unknowing, but rather an unformulated and unrecognized form of knowing" (Askay & Farquhar, 2005, p. 299).

"Introspection, Empathy and Psychoanalysis" had claimed that the only data of interest to psychoanalysis were experiential data accessible only through empathy and introspection. In other words, he announced a phenomenological psychoanalysis. Likewise, Atwood, Stolorow, Brandchaft, and Orange (Atwood & Stolorow, 1984; Orange et al., 1997; Stolorow & Atwood, 1992; Stolorow et al., 1987; Stolorow et al., 2002) have developed a psychoanalytic phenomenology whose spirit, I believe, Merleau-Ponty would have found close to his own embodied intersubjectivity.

Like Merleau-Ponty and unlike some current users of the term *intersubjectivity* as a developmental achievement, we psychoanalytic intersubjectivists find ourselves always already woven into the many intersubjective systems that give birth to us, and within which we develop. Like Merleau-Ponty, and with Winnicott, we argue that there can be no fully individual experience: "There is no such thing as an infant, there is no such thing as a patient, there is no such thing as the patient's or the analyst's shame" (Orange, 2008c, p. 90). Here is Merleau-Ponty's version:

> Even that universal meditation which cuts the philosopher off from his nation, his friendships, his prejudices, his empirical being, the world in short, and which seems to leave him in complete isolation, is in reality an act, the spoken world, and consequently dialogue . . . the social word [is] a permanent field or dimension of existence; I may well turn away from it but not cease to be situated relatively to it. (1945/2002, pp. 420–421)

CONCLUSION: A CLOSELY WOVEN FABRIC

We clinicians too are interwoven into the flesh of the world, to use the words of Merleau-Ponty's posthumously published *The Visible and the Invisible* (Merleau-Ponty, 1964/1968, 1968). The chiasm, or intertwining, both weighs us down with sedimented meanings—the organizing principles and emotional convictions—and gives us hope. We know that "the war has taken place" (Merleau-Ponty, 1964b) and that we are implicated. But because we are connected "all the way down," because the real is a closely woven fabric, because there is nothing before intersubjectivity, we can believe that our common humanity can save us. In Merleau-Ponty's words, "The momentum of existence towards others, towards the future, towards the world can be restored as a river unfreezes" (1945/2002, p. 191).

5

EMMANUEL LEVINAS
Trauma and the Face of the Other

If one could possess, grasp, and know the other, it would not be other. Possessing, knowing, and grasping are synonyms of power.

—Levinas

The Jew has the feeling that his obligations with respect to the other come before his obligations to God, or more precisely that the other is the voice of high places, even of the sacred.

—Levinas, quoted in Malka

It is through the condition of being a hostage that there can be pity, compassion, pardon, and proximity in the world—even the little there is, even the simple "after you, sir."

—Levinas

Like Merleau-Ponty, Emmanuel Levinas lived in France, wrote in French, and began his philosophical life immersed in Husserl's phenomenology. Unlike Merleau-Ponty, Levinas had little interest in scientific psychology, and even less in the café culture of French intellectuals around Jean-Paul Sartre. Instead, a traumatized survivor, he searched the lifeworlds of both Western philosophy and Judaism, and discovered an ethics to disturb all our settled theories and to transform our personal and clinical lives.

LIFE AND WORK[*]

Emmanuel Levinas was part philosopher, part Talmudic scholar, and part prophet. Born in Lithuania in 1906, Levinas and his family moved to Ukraine in 1915, refugees from the German occupation, and returned to Lithuania in 1920. He studied in Strasbourg, where Bergson's philosophy of lived duration (*la durée*) became an enduring influence for him. In 1928–1929, he studied phenomenology in Freiburg with Husserl and Heidegger. From Husserl he learned the relentless focus on lived experience (Levinas & Nemo, 1982/1985), and he remained a lifelong phenomenologist: "The phenomenological method enables us to find meaning within our lived experience" (Cohen, 1986, p. 14). His doctoral dissertation, *The Theory of Intuition in Husserl's Phenomenology* (1973), introduced the method and spirit of phenomenology to France, where it spread to Sartre and Merleau-Ponty. Like many others, the young Levinas was caught up in the fever generated by Heidegger's early philosophy of being-in-the-world, and throughout his life Levinas valued Heidegger's account of affectivity, or *Befindlichkeit* (Heidegger, 1927/1962, p. 1074; see also Gendlin, 1979, p. 1112), for its worlded relationality. Already a serious admirer of Bergson's account of *durée* in *Time and Free Will* (Bergson & Pogson, 1910), the young Levinas was also drawn to Heidegger's understanding of human being (Dasein) as temporality. He spoke of Heidegger's *Being and Time* (1967) as comparable to the work of Plato and Hegel, but, shocked and horrified, he abandoned his book on Heidegger when that philosopher joined the Nazis and, as rector, tried to impose their program on Freiburg University in 1933–1934. In 1931 Levinas became a French citizen and in 1939 enrolled in the officer corps where he worked as an interpreter of Russian and German. In 1940 he was imprisoned in a labor camp near Hannover for 5 years until the war's end, while his wife and daughter were hidden by nuns. His status as a French officer kept him from transfer to the death camps, but as a Jew, he was made to work harder than the others. Only the camp dog, Bobby, he later wrote, welcomed the Jewish prisoners as much as the others (Levinas, 2001, p. 92). His entire Lithuanian family was murdered.[†] His life was, he later said, "dominated by the presentiment and the memory of the Nazi horror" (Levinas, 1990, p. 291).

---

[*] Biographical information comes mainly from two sources: Malka (2006) and Critchley and Bernasconi (2002).

[†] Jean Greisch told Salomon Malka, author of a gripping biography of Levinas, that he remembered "Levinas telling me how surprised he was that thinkers could be amazed by the fact that there is something rather than nothing . . . to his mind, the fact that in a world as cruel as ours, something like the miracle of kindness could appear was infinitely more worthy of amazement" (Malka, 2006, p. 171).

After the war, he directed the École Normale Israelite Orientale (ENIO) in Paris, a school for Sephardic Jews. He studied the Talmud with the mysterious "Monsieur Chouchani" (also the teacher of Elie Wiesel). He became a revered teacher of the Talmud, but also wrote philosophical works. *Totality and Infinity: An Essay on Exteriority* (1969), his first full attempt to articulate his point of view, was published in 1960, and earned him the *doctorat d'état*. By 1967 he was professor at the University of Paris, along with Paul Ricoeur. Having taken into account Derrida's critique—you are using Heidegger's language to refute Heidegger ("Violence and Metaphysics," Derrida, 1967/1978)*— he produced his second magnum opus, *Otherwise than Being, or Beyond Essence* (1974/1981). Many books and lectures later, he died in 1995. Interest in his work has grown immensely since his death, in part because an ethical void was left by postmodernism, in part due to the prominence of the Habermasian (Habermas, 1981/1984, 1983/1990) and Rawlsian (Rawls, 1971) rationalist theories of equal treatment justice. They had unfortunately neglected to include an ethics of the infinite value of every individual human being. The much-needed work of Levinas addresses this gap.

THE "BIG IDEA" OF EMMANUEL LEVINAS

The "big idea" of Emmanuel Levinas was, in the words of Simon Critchley,[†] "that ethics is first philosophy, where ethics is understood as a radically asymmetrical relation of infinite responsibility to the other person" (Critchley, 2002, p. 6). In Levinas's own words, "the ethical relation is not grafted on to an antecedent relation of cognition; it is a foundation and not a superstructure" (1987, p. 56). To understand this idea, we must remember that Heidegger, for whom ontology, the study of being, was everything, used his philosophy to support the regime that imprisoned and enslaved Levinas for 5 years and murdered all his family. Though Levinas continued to regard Heidegger as "a philosophical intelligence among the greatest and fewest," he always also commented on "the irreversible abomination attached to National Socialism in

---

* According to Derrida, *Totality and Infinity* contained an internal contradiction: It used Heideggerian ontological language, like all generalizing ("totalizing" in Levinasian language) philosophies inherently violent. At the same time it attempts to propound an ethics beyond the ontology that reduces the other (*Autrui*) to the same (totality, categories, conceptions). In other words, Derrida used Levinas's own ethics as a critique of the way Levinas was presenting his views.

† I am more than grateful to Simon Critchley for his hospitality in making Levinas accessible to me. It is a response that leaves the neighbor changed.

which the brilliant man could have, in one way or another, it does not matter how, taken part" (Malka, 2006). Levinas became convinced that something "otherwise" than being or knowledge must be fundamental. Already in his title, *Totality and Infinity*, he contrasted what he called "totalizing," or treating others as something to be studied or comprehended, with responding to the face of the other. This irreducible "face" always transcends our concepts, representations, and ideas: "The way in which other presents himself, exceeding *the idea of the other in me*, we here name face" (Levinas, 1964/1969, p. 50). The other (*Autrui*, the human other) presents me with an infinite demand for protection and care. The face says: you shall not kill (*tu ne tueras point*). You shall not allow me to die alone.

Levinas contrasted his sense of the ethical "height" of the other, or *Autrui*, with description of the same (*le même*):

> The neighbor concerns me before all assumption, all commitment consented to or refused. I am bound to him, him who is, however, the first one on the scene, not signaled, unparalleled; I am bound to him before any liaison contracted. He orders me before being recognized. Here there is a relation of kinship, outside of all biology, "against all logic." It is not because the neighbor would be recognized as belonging to the same genus as me that he concerns me. He is precisely *other*. The community with him begins in my obligation to him. The neighbor is a brother. (Levinas, 1974/1981, p. 87)*

Here we find immediately the difficulties in reading Levinas: (a) He did not argue like a philosopher, but pronounced like a prophet; (b) his writing is intentionally metaphoric, intending with hyperbole to shock us, dislodging our previous certainties and complacencies; and (c) his unusual use of familiar words makes rereading necessary.† At the same time, his writing, enigmatic and challenging like much rabbinic commentary on the Talmud, richly repays rereading and discussion.

Returning to content, we find the "other" contrasted with the "same." The other infinitely transcends the totalizing representations that reduce the other to the same—this is the theme of *Totality and Infinity*. Contrast, for example, 2008 U.S. presidential candidate John McCain's use of the locution "that one" to refer to his political opponent with the response to Autrui‡ who addresses me, who is my brother. Every

---

* Though Levinas seriously tried to keep his philosophical and "confessional" writings separate, the resonances come through, as here with the biblical sense of *covenant*.

† The Glossary contains entries for some of these words.

‡ Levinas used both upper and lower case with no apparent method, so I have decided to follow his translators and many commentators, and use the lowercase *other* in English and the uppercase *Autrui* in French.

reduction—by systematizing, classifying, pointing, even describing—is, for Levinas, a violence, a violation, a form of murder. The neighbor, instead, exposes me "to the summons of this responsibility as though placed under a blazing sun that eradicates every residue of mystery, every ulterior motive, every loosening of the thread that would allow evasion" (Levinas, 1996, p. 104). The response must be "*Me voici*" (me here): I am indeed my brother's keeper, and there is no escape.

The relation to the other (*Autrui*) creates what Levinas called a "curvature of intersubjective space" (Levinas, 1961/1969, p. 291). What can this mean? The ethical relation is not between equals, but is asymmetrical;* that is, from "inside that relation, as it takes place, at this very moment, you place an obligation on me that makes you more than me, more than my equal" (Critchley & Bernasconi, 2002, p. 14). Because I cannot expect the same responsibility without limits of the other toward whom I bear it, society is needed:

> The other stands in a relationship with the third party [society], for whom I cannot entirely answer, even if I alone answer, before any question, for my neighbor . . . Justice, society, the State and its institutions, exchanges and work are comprehensible on the basis of proximity. This means that nothing is outside of the control of the responsibility of the one for the other. (Levinas, 1974/1981, pp. 157-159)

In other words, although we need law and justice and equal treatment ethics, the fundamental[†] ethical relation of proximity to the neighbor is so radically tilted and irreversible as not to seem equal in any phenomenologically describable way.

To understand what Levinas had in mind, we must remember that he told us in many places how decisive for his thought was the trauma of what he called "Hitlerism" (Levinas, 1934/1990) and what Derrida often called "the worst." Levinas's second important philosophical work, *Otherwise than Being* (1998c), is dedicated "To the memory of those who were closest among the six million assassinated by the National Socialists, and of the millions on millions of all confessions and all nations, victims of the same hatred of the other man, the same anti–semitism" (Levinas, 1981). He followed this dedication with the names, in Hebrew, of his own family members who were murdered.

---

* Compare with Aron (1996) and Buber (1923/1970, 1999).
† Here we can see that Levinas refused or abandoned the complete antifoundationalism of Nietzsche, Heidegger, and the French postmodernists. His concept of infinity—the unbounded responsibility or infinite demand placed on me by the face of the other—owes its inspiration, by his own account, to that of Descartes (1641/1996).

Two important characteristics appear in these inscriptions. First, Levinas wrote from personal experience, though shared with unthinkably many others, of horror and loss beyond our ordinary conceptions of trauma. One way to read his philosophy is to read him as a traumatized person, including residues in his work of traumatically generated dualisms (Orange, in press) and political blindspots of traumatic origin.* But there is also a blazing-sun clarity in the testimony of the traumatized, as we will see below. Second, Levinas saw clearly that every form of hatred of otherness shares the violence of anti-Semitism. Beyond his own traumatic history, he saw every reduction of the other to the same (his language in *Totality and Infinity*) as murderous. For him, concepts like "positive aggression" (Perls, 1969) or engaging the patient's aggression (Bachant & Richards, 1993; Levenson, 1996) would be ethically unthinkable. They would signify a return to the ominous rumbling of the impersonal and reductive *il y a* (there is), embodied in the *Stalag*, a world without the "you may not kill me." There, Levinas (1963/1990) noted, "None of the generosity which the German term "*es gibt*" [there is] is said [by Heidegger] to contain revealed itself between 1933 and 1945. This must be said!" (p. 292).

In a devastating critique of objectifying reductions, Levinas (1963/1990) wrote:

> Knowledge reveals, names and consequently classifies. Speech addresses itself to a face. Knowledge seizes hold of its object. It possesses it. Possession denies the independence of being, without destroying that being—it denies and maintains. But the face, for its part, is inviolable; those eyes, which are absolutely without protection, the most naked part of the human body, none the less offer an absolute resistance to possession, an absolute resistance in which the temptation to murder is inscribed: the temptation of absolute negation. (p. 8)

Instead, irreducibility is indispensable to the "big idea" of Emmanuel Levinas. The face into which I look, and which places its infinite demand on me, is not just a mask for the brain, or for some Plotinian emanation, or for a Heideggerian unveiling of Being. Instead, for Levinas, as for all philosophical phenomenologists, experience, especially of the other, escapes all formulations, representations, and mechanical descriptions. It is elusive, ungraspable, and inaccessible (Zahavi, 2005). In his later work,

---

* Levinas's political conservatism—his refusal to criticize Israel for its destruction of Chatila and Sabra in 1982, his idealization of France, his support for the Soviet Union even after its demise, his patriarchalism—illustrates this concept of political blind spots traumatically generated. A fine account can be found in Caygill (2002).

especially in *Otherwise than Being* (1979/1981), Levinas contrasted the living Saying (*le Dire*) with the Said (*le Dit*), the inevitable but still problematic reductions and objectifications in what is said* (Levinas & Nemo, 1982/1985, p. 88). The face, in Critchley's words, "is not something I see, but something I speak to" (Critchley, 2002, p. 12). According to Levinas, "the *saying* is the fact that before the face I do not simply remain there contemplating it, I respond to it" (Levinas & Nemo, 1982/1985, p. 88).

My response to the face is simply "*me voici*,"† not "here I am" as it is usually translated, but rather, as Paul Ricoeur (1940/1992) pointed out, "it's me here." Ricoeur thought it no mistake that the accusative form appealed to Levinas: The face of the other accuses me, and makes subjectivity either irrelevant or nonexistent. "Since the initiative belongs wholly to the Other, it is in the accusative—a mode well named—that the I is met by the injunction and made capable of answering, again in the accusative: 'It's me here!'" (Ricoeur, 1940/1992, pp. 337–338). As me, the face of the other calls me, demands from me, takes me hostage, persecutes me. Response is my refusal to be unmoved, or indifferent, to the face of the other, to the other's "useless suffering" (Levinas, 1991/1981). Sometimes Levinas implied that I cannot be indifferent, that I am held hostage, but he knew very well that many did not respond. This "cannot" avoid responsibility must refer to the ethical demand. What I am or need, or how I feel toward the other, is, for Levinasian ethics, not in question.

TRAUMA AND TESTIMONY

Trauma, an everyday word in the vocabulary of many clinicians, takes on a surprising sense in the work of Levinas—even for those of us who think of trauma as lived memory rather than as event. We should of course hear his own terrible history in his use of *trauma* and *traumatism*. As if we could put aside his massive losses of family, let us return with him to Fallingbostel, the prisoner–of–war camp near Hannover, where Levinas was imprisoned for most of the war. Because he wrote so little about his captivity—fearing probably to reduce trauma to something known, to the Said—I will quote him at length:

> There were seventy of us in a forestry commando unit for Jewish prisoners of war in Nazi Germany. An extraordinary coincidence

---

* I am reminded of clinical situations in which something one says seems to both parties just right at that moment (the Saying), but written down, or even just remembered a few days later, it seems trite, objectifying, even humiliating. It has become the reductive, representing, objectifying Said.

† There is also a biblical resonance here for Levinas, who often said this in Hebrew, *hineni*.

was the fact that camp bore the number 1492, the year of the expulsion of the Jews from Spain under the Catholic Ferdinand V. The French uniform still protected us from Hitlerian violence. But the other men, called free, who had dealings with us or gave us work or orders or even a smile—and the children and women who passed by and sometimes raised their eyes—stripped us of our human skin. We were subhuman, a gang of apes. A small inner murmur, the strength and wretchedness of persecuted people, reminded us of our essence as thinking creatures, but we were no longer part of the world. Our comings and goings, our sorrow and laughter, illnesses and distractions, the work of our hands and anguish of our eyes, the letters we received from France and those accepted for our families—all that passed in parenthesis. We were beings entrapped in their species; despite all their vocabulary, beings without language. Racism is not a biological concept; anti–Semitism is the archetype of all internment. . . . It shuts people away in a class, deprives them of expression and condemns them to being "signifiers without a signified". . . . How can we deliver a message about our humanity which, from behind the bars of quotation marks, will come across as anything other than monkey talk?

And then, about halfway through our long captivity, for a few short weeks, before the sentinels chased him away, a wandering dog entered our lives. One day he came to meet this rabble as we returned under guard from work. He survived in some wild patch in the region of the camp. But we called him Bobby, an exotic name, as one does with a cherished dog. He would appear at morning assembly and was waiting for us as we returned, jumping up and down and barking in delight. For him, there was no doubt that we were men. . . . This dog was the last Kantian in Nazi Germany, without the brain needed to universalize maxims and drives. (Levinas, 1963/1990, pp. 152–153)

Let us give this passage a double reading, though more Levinasian than Derridean.* Here we find the traumatized speaking the unspeakable (Orange, in press) and bearing witness (Orange, 1995) in the more traditional sense in clinical work that recognizes trauma as experience, not event. Levinas speaks as one of the humans reduced to apes, the same, and of the joy that even Bobby could find in responding to the human other. He further, telling this story, provides a kind of testimony that could be corroborated or not, that could be reduced to "holocaust memoir," to "the facts." Precisely because of the danger of reducing

---

* Derrida's fascinating and subversive "double reading"—of Levinas, for example, in "Violence and Metaphysics"—includes a "straight" exegesis of a text, followed by one that shows its self–undermining character. See Derrida (1978).

the Shoah, he normally avoided speaking of it, preferring to allow the unspeakable its hallowed ground.

At the same time, we can read this passage using Levinas's own senses of "traumatism" (Critchley, 1999) and testimony. For Levinas, trauma is the experience of responsibility for the destitute neighbor, for his or her suffering (Chanter, 1997). The suffering other holds me hostage. Levinas (2000) asked, "So, does the trauma of the other [*l'autre*] come from the Other [*d'Autrui*]? Is the nothingness of death not the very nudity of the neighbor's face? You shall not commit murder is the nudity of the face" (pp. 116–117). My survivor's guilt is a traumatism, a condition produced by traumatic substitution for the suffering neighbor, but a substitution that always comes too late. As Levinas so often quoted from Dostoyevsky: "Every one of us is guilty before all, for everyone and everything, and I more than others . . . an original traumatism" (Levinas et al., 1996, p. 90), not dependent on particular events. The ethical subject arises in its response to alterity, unconsciously (Critchley, 1999). Speaking of Levinas's relation to psychoanalysis, Critchley continues:

> The Levinasian subject is a traumatized self, a subject that is con-
> stituted through a self-relation that is experienced as a lack, where
> the self is experienced as the inassumable source of what is lacking
> from the ego—a subject of melancholia, then. But this is a *good
> thing*. It is only because the subject is unconsciously constituted
> through the trauma of contact with the real that we might have
> the audacity to speak of goodness, transcendence, compassion . . . .
> Without trauma, there would be no ethics in Levinas's particular
> sense of the word. (p. 195)

This traumatized subject in turn—no, in this very moment—bears witness, testifies, to infinity, the transcendence of the suffering other.

Testimony, the original Saying, reverses the usual production of a report, a "Said" that invites cross-checking. Responding to the other's destitution, my testimony testifies to the Infinite, to the transcendence of the other over me. We testify to the glory of the Infinite when we welcome the other in her or his need. We are not saying "I believe in God"—there is too much "I" here—but rather, in the face of the neighbor, God "comes to mind" (*vient à l'idée*). So testimony refuses to reduce the other to an instance of trauma; instead, we traumatized witnesses take on the suffering and death of the other as our own responsibility. "Ethics," in Critchley's (1999) words, "is not a spectator sport; rather it is my experience of a claim or demand that I both cannot fully meet and cannot avoid" (p. 66).

In clinical work, such a traumatic testimony occurs commonly. So many colleagues and supervisees tell me that they find themselves traumatized by their work. Only since reading Levinas have I found a way to give a sense to the therapist's traumatic experience. When a patient, seriously mistreated by a previous therapist, comes to me, the crime becomes mine. Unless I respond in this spirit, the Levinasian and Dostoyevskian spirit, my patient has no chance. If I refuse to take on the guilt, I implicitly blame the patient for the horror perpetrated by my colleague, and abandon the neighbor to die alone. This willingness to take on my survivor guilt, I believe, must extend to all my clinical work if I am not to reduce the other to the same and use diagnostic categories in the service of this reduction. More discussion of a Levinasian therapeutics follows below.

It is tempting to give an extended Levinasian reading—relying on his language of traumatism and of testimony—to a recent documentary called *Inheritance* (PBS, 2008). Instead, a too brief synopsis will have to suffice. Monika Hertwig, a German woman of about 60 (born late in 1945), contacts Helen Jonas, an American Jewish survivor, perhaps 75. Monika has gradually come to know she is the daughter of Amon Göth, commandant of Plaszow Concentration Camp. When she sees his full brutality in *Schindler's List,* she originally hates Steven Spielberg for what he has made her see, but then comes to want to meet Helen, Göth's victim and former house slave. Both travel to the camp site and then to the villa where Helen, brutalized herself, had watched Göth randomly kill people for fun. Both women are so traumatized that they can scarcely bear each other's suffering. The faces of both, but especially of Monika, embody "destitution." The subjectivity of each is a Levinasian subjection to the misery of the other. But it seems that, from both sides, they cannot fully respond to the other, yet both are courageous enough not to avoid the attempt. Subjectivity is never enough; the ethical demand reaches to infinity.

THE SUBJECT AFTER LEVINAS

The Levinasian subject is thus possessed in herself or himself only of a minimal, even pathetic, subjectivity. A respondent—not a protagonist or even an agent—the Levinasian subject comes to life, more or less fleetingly, in subjection to the neighbor. I come to being as a substitute for the widow, the orphan, and the stranger (Levinas, 1996). I am hostage to the other, without self–being.

In striking contrast to Heidegger's designation of subjectivity as *Jemeinigkeit,* or possession of my own being as my own, Levinas deposes this sovereign self:

For ethical thought, on the contrary, *the self*, as this primacy of what is mine, is *hateful** . . . . I am defined as a subjectivity, as a singular person, as an "I," precisely because I am exposed to the other. It is my inescapable and incontrovertible answerability to the other that makes me an individual "I." So that I become a responsible or ethical "I" to the extent that I agree to depose or dethrone myself—to abdicate my position of centrality—in favor of the vulnerable other. (Levinas, in Cohen, 1986, pp. 26–27)

Responding to the destitute face of the neighbor, I become a "first person" only as a "first responder," one who finds in my own empty hands the resources to answer the call.

What happens to intersubjectivity in the asymmetry of Levinasian ethics? Husserl's conception of the intersubjective constitution of experience long interested Levinas. Also we have seen that Merleau-Ponty (1964c) pictured intersubjectivity as two hands touching in a handshake, intertwined in a chiasm, where we are "like organs of one single intercorporeality" (p. 168). Levinas (1998b), however, understood intersubjectivity as the asymmetrical "interhuman" in which suffering is "meaningful in me, useless in the other" (p. 100). In his "Useless Suffering" (1991/1998b), preparing to declare theodicy† (defense of deity against the problem of evil) an unthinkable scandal after a century of "unutterable suffering," he explained:

There is a radical difference between *the suffering in the other*, where it is unforgivable to *me*, solicits me and calls me and suffering *in me*, my own experience of suffering, whose constitutional or congenital uselessness can take on a meaning, the only one of which suffering is capable, in becoming a suffering for the suffering (inexorable though it may be) of someone else. (p. 94)

This clinician hears in these words both a permission and a responsibility to understand my own traumatic suffering as meaningful insofar as it enables me to respond to, and to suffer for, my destitute neighbor—as Levinas often said, the widow, the orphan, and the stranger. Insofar as my patients come to me suffering, naked, impoverished, my own suffering can take on meaning.

Where Brentano and Husserl had thought empathy—as a form of intentionality (see Glossary)—could provide authentic connection to

---

* Levinas liked to cite Pascal: "The I is hateful" (*Le moi est haissable*) (Pascal , trans. 2008).

† Susan Neiman (2002) notes that Levinas extended his critique of "theodicy" to all attempts to explain away evil, not only to religious arguments. Richard Bernstein (2002) develops this idea in a valuable chapter on Levinas.

the other, Levinas claimed that another grasped by me is no longer other. "My encounter with foreign subjectivity," says Zahavi (2005), "is not conditioned by anything in my power, but has the character of a visitation, an epiphany, or a revelation" (p. 172). It "interrupts and disrupts my dogmatic slumber by putting me into question" (p. 232, n. 16). Late in life, asked whether the other is not also responsible toward me, Levinas responded:

> Perhaps, but that is *his* affair . . . the intersubjective relation is a non–symmetrical relation . . . I am responsible for the other without waiting for reciprocity, were I to die for it. Reciprocity is *his* affair. It is precisely insofar as the relationship between the Other and me is not reciprocal that I am subjection to the Other; and I am "subject" essentially in this sense. It is I who support all. (Levinas & Nemo, 1982/1985, p. 98)

So Levinasian intersubjectivity is no Hegelian struggle and has nothing to do with the master–slave dialectic or with a totalizing system. Instead, it means that, as in Husserl, Merleau-Ponty, and in our intersubjective systems psychoanalysis, the subject is constituted—the passive/receptive voice is deliberate here—the subject is constituted in its responsiveness to the other.

AUTHENTICITY OR SINCERITY: A QUESTION FOR PSYCHOTHERAPISTS

Authenticity—highly valued in contemporary psychoanalysis—appears in the work of Emmanuel Levinas only as a target of critique. But seemingly related words like *sincerity* are prominent. Why? The concern with authenticity as a moral category would seem to have begun with Nietzsche, whose philosophical career could be seen as one of relentless unmasking of pretensions, especially philosophical and religious. He saw traditional morality as an inauthentic refusal to take responsibility for one's own life, and to move "beyond good and evil" (Nietzsche, 1886/1966, p. 906). He advocated a self-chosen life, similar to Heideggerian "resoluteness," a prominent feature of *Being and Time*, and infamously echoed in Heidegger's 1933 *Rektoratsrede* (inaugural lecture for a new university rector/president in which Heidegger outlined his program for bringing Freiburg University in line [*Gleichschaltung*] with the intentions of the Third Reich).

In ordinary usage, of course, *authentic* means genuine or true, as opposed to fake or phony. It is a word heard often on "Antiques

Roadshow." For those of us, however, who came of age in the 1960s and 1970s, full of European existentialism, "authenticity" seems to come from Heidegger. His word, *Eigentlichkeit,* always translated into English as "authenticity," primarily reflects the German words *eigen* (one's own), and to a lesser extent the question *"Eigentlich?"* (Really?). Thus, authentic being is what really comes from Dasein's (the human being's) ownness and lives from its possibilities. Inauthenticity, by contrast, is the thoughtless mode of the crowd, of the "they" (*das Man*), into which we feel endlessly drawn and into which we are always "falling," as if into sin. Authenticity, instead, means the unfolding of one's own possibilities of being, and describes the subjectivity of being-in-the-world not absorbed into the crowd, the anyone, the neutral they (*das Man*). Authenticity sounds truthful, agentic, and courageous, in Heidegger's words, resolute.

Unfortunately authenticity concerns only Dasein's being and has little to do with the other or with any ethical obligation. Granted, Heidegger's account of Dasein's being-with (*Mitsein*) contains an idea that Dasein can assist in the opening of others to their authentic (own) possibilities. But this seems a weak kind of relatedness that does not see Dasein itself as intersubjectively constituted. In the view of psychiatrist-philosopher Ludwig Binswanger, Roger Frie (2002) tells us, "The difficulty lay in the fact that Dasein achieved its authenticity, or self-understanding, in essential isolation from others. In other words, Heidegger does not include the possibility of achieving authenticity through dialogue with another" (pp. 645–646). The ideal of authenticity is ethically indiscriminate, and does not even include the famous "do no harm." It was unfortunately quite consistent with Nazi attitudes as many have noted (Adorno, 1964/1973; Bumbach, 2003; and Vogel, 1994). Authenticity could not be an ideal for those devastated by the "worst."

By contrast, Levinas, for whom ethics preceded and even obviated Heidegger's fundamental ontology, proposed a radical ethical asymmetry. Responding to the face of the other constitutes the infinitely responsible ethical subjectivity or subjection. The other (*Autrui*) is above me, transcends me, holds me hostage, traumatizes me. The authentic expression of my own being never comes into consideration in the work of Levinas. Instead my response to the other's need must always be the sincere and hospitable *"Me voici."*

But what is this sincerity and what is this hospitality, and how can these be ethically demanded of us? In the work of Levinas (1981), sincerity and hospitality are two of many ways of Saying (*le Dire*), that is, what can never be reduced to the Said (*le Dit*). Here are some admittedly difficult words of Levinas:

> Saying opens me to the other (*autrui*) before saying what is said, before the said uttered in this sincerity forms a screen between me and the other. A saying without words, but not with empty hands. If silence speaks, it is . . . through the hyperbolic passivity of giving, which is prior to all willing thematization. Saying bears witness to the other (*autrui*) of the Infinite which rends me, which in the Saying awakens me. (Levinas et al., 1996, p. 145)

Sincerity, Levinas seemed to be saying, is our open-handed and open-hearted response to the other. Far from the abstinence and nongratification of traditional psychoanalysis, we say to the devastated and destitute other: Here is bread, here is wine, eat and drink. Nothing—no reduction to theory, category, or "thematization"—precedes this sincere offering of hospitality. Utterly passive before the other's face, I allow the other to tear me open. "Saying is what makes the self–exposure of sincerity possible; it is a way of giving everything, of not keeping anything for oneself" (Levinas, in Cohen, 1986, p. 28).

The words of Levinas remind me of those of Georges Bernanos in his *Journal d'un Curé de Campagne* ([The Diary of a Country Priest] 1936/2002):

> "Be at peace," I told her. And she had knelt to receive this peace. May she keep it for ever. It will be I that give it her. Oh, miracle— thus to be able to give what we ourselves do not possess, sweet miracle of our empty hands! Hope which was shriveling in my heart flowered again in hers. (p. 180)

The priest has lost his own faith, but evokes it in the dying woman, much as the sincere gesture/words of hospitality do in Levinas. In my clinical experience, I am often called by the other's need, the other's Face, to find a way to give what I do not possess with hands both empty and not. Critics may call this inauthenticity; Levinas would call it responsibility, sincerity, hospitality.

LEVINAS AND BUBER

Closest to and yet different from this Levinasian ethics was the philosophy of Martin Buber. Whether Buber and Levinas ever met face-to-to face, their sources (Rosenzweig, 1921/2005) and concerns to a great extent overlapped (Levinas & Nemo, 1982/1985), but Levinas expressed in several places his strong ambivalence toward Buber (Atterton, Calanco, & Friedman, 2004; Levinas, 1987/1993). Levinas always credited Buber

as "pioneer" of his own "big idea": "that the presence of an interlocutor to me cannot be reduced to the presence of an object that my gaze
determines and upon which it makes predicative judgments" (Levinas
& Smith, 1993, p. 14). Nor can the neighbor be absorbed into me or vice
versa; we meet each other in what Levinas calls irreducible proximity,
relation to the neighbor. Buber's I, explains Levinas,

> in its relation with the Thou is further related to itself by means
> of the Thou, i.e., it is related to the Thou as to someone who in
> turn relates itself to the I, as though it came into delicate contact
> with himself through the skin of the Thou . . . in the *Umfassung*
> [inclusion] the I sharply maintains its active reality. (Schilpp et al.,
> 1967, p. 142)

For both, the realm of the interhuman* was both the sphere of the ethical and our only access to the divine. Buber's life of dialogue was an
appeal and invitation to a dialogic form of human connection, and
a passionate call to awareness of the many ways in which we reduce
and objectify each other. "Nothing," Levinas (1987/1994) said of Buber,
"could limit the homage due him" (p. 41).

Still, besides his discomfort at times with what he took to be Buber's
mystical (Hasidic) bent, he also had two specific and ongoing objections to the way Buber conceived the I-Thou (*moi-toi* for Levinas)
relation.† First, Levinas found Buber's "meeting" too formal. In other
words, the other has no unique and irreplaceable qualities in Buber's
account; instead it could be anyone, replaceable and interchangeable.
Buber's interhuman has none of the concrete aspect, the immediacy
and importunity that leads Levinas to reach out to the other and say,
"Drink!" (Critchley, 1991). But Buber thought Levinas misunderstood
him and that solicitude could not substitute for meeting: "He may
clothe the naked and feed the hungry all day and it will remain difficult
for him to say a true Thou" (Schilpp et al., 1967, p. 723).

Even worse, according to Levinas, Buber's emphases on symme-
try, reversibility, and equality render invisible the originary‡ "height"
or transcendence of the other over me. "There is no initial equality"

---

* "The temporality of the interhuman opens up the meaning of otherness and the otherness of meaning" (Levinas, in Cohen, 1986, p. 21).

† Levinas increasingly used the *moi* in the lower case (Chanter, 1997). I think he wanted to
 emphasize the insignificance of the subject as compared with the "height" of the neighbor. Chanter lists Levinas's priorities: "Responsibility before freedom, ethics before uni-
 versal ontology, infinity before totality, the other before me, passivity before power, the
 'here I am' of witness before the 'I think' of representation" (p. 21).

‡ Not *original*, as in "innovative;" but *originary*, as in referring back to origins, as Levinas
 liked to say, to the "immemorial past."

(Levinas, 1993, p. 43). Buber's dialogue could, he thought, degenerate into a form of I-It relation. Instead, proclaimed Levinas, the neighbor has a claim on me that exceeds and precedes everything. The face of the other creates my unlimited and gratuitous (not dependent on acts of freedom) responsibility that cannot be reduced or displaced. As noted above, I am hostage to the other, who is always my guest in the response of hospitality. Instead of a Buberian I that reaches toward a You, Levinas begins with the other whose face places the double demand on me: You must not kill me, and you must protect and care for me. You must not abandon me in my need. (It is easy to hear Levinas addressing the "innocent" bystanders who had watched their Jewish neighbors deported).

Why should this dispute matter to us psychotherapists, especially when these two thinkers held so much in common? First let us remember that Buber made some exceptions to his requirements for dialogic reciprocity and equality. Teachers, pastors, therapists, and parents, he thought, bear a responsibility to those in their care that need not, indeed should not, be reciprocated. The difference is, perhaps, that Levinas saw all ethical relation as asymmetrical, as placing an infinite and irreducible responsibility on me. For clinicians, Buber appeals to our sense of vocation; Levinas would place our work in the "otherwise," in the beyond, in the transcendence of the ethical relation itself. Neither would allow us to expect or demand recognition from our patients.* Both leave us quite often with King Lear's problem: "How sharper than a serpent's tooth it is to have a thankless child." We are, after all, both would agree, our brother's keepers.† But Buber found "the between" primary; for Levinas, the face of the suffering neighbor precedes all relation.

Second, in the plausible view of Robert Bernasconi (Atterton et al., 2004), Levinas in his later years appreciated Buber more and valued his inspiration. He began to accord to Buber the status of an ethical thinker, as he, in Bernasconi's words, awakened "the 'saying' of Buber from his said" (p. 91). Perhaps no longer needing to define his own views in terms of this opposition, he could more easily say "we" to Buber. We clinicians sometimes find a similar softening toward the giants we have formerly needed to oppose, as do our patients with us.

---

* Both philosophers have a peculiar relationship to the feminine: Buber's second person *Du* has no gender, while Levinas's ethical subjectivity, as well as his other, seem always to be the masculine *il*. See Irigaray and Whitford (1991).

† Levinas, however, had no place for any form of recognition in his view of relatedness. He saw recognition as inevitably reducing the other to a totalizing same, as a form of cognition, knowing, domination, and violence. Elsewhere, I have contrasted Benjamin's notion of mutual recognition with other possibilities (Orange, 2008b).

A LEVINASIAN THERAPEUTICS?

So how does "my brother's keeper"—for whom the neighbor always has priority—work as a clinical guide? At least three ideas express this primacy of ethics for Levinas: irreducibility, proximity, and substitution. We shall consider each in turn. We can then ask if the Levinasian ethic demands too much of the clinician who would survive to work another day.

Irreducibility is indispensable to the "big idea" of Emmanuel Levinas. The face into which I look, and which places its infinite demand on me, is not just a facade for the nervous system or for its control center. Instead, for Levinas as for all philosophical phenomenologists, experience—especially of the other—escapes all formulations, representations, and mechanical descriptions. The said always reduces the saying, and the saying challenges this reductive objectifying. (Wittgenstein similarly had contrasted what could be said—the unimportant—with what could only be shown. I think the Levinasian "saying" "here I am" to the other resembles Wittgenstein's showing).

Proximity, another key word in Levinas, means to him both the nearness and distance of our relation to the other.* *Autrui* is near because she or he leaves me no ethical space in which to turn away and distance because he or she is standing infinitely above and beyond me. "In proximity is heard a command come as though from an immemorial past,[†] which was never present, began in no freedom. This *way* of the neighbor is face" (Levinas, 1974/1981, p. 88). Thus, my singularity is not a kind of self-identification. Instead, in Bernasconi's summary, it is unutterable, cramped, ill at ease, it is exposure to wounding and outrage, unable to take a distance from itself, radically responsible for the other prior to any contact or choice (Critchley & Bernasconi, 2002). It is "uniqueness without interiority, me without rest in itself, hostage of all, turned away from itself in each movement of its return to itself" (Levinas, 1987, p. 150). Levinasian proximity, as the saying goes, afflicts the comfortable.

Levinasian ethics, though extreme in one sense, need not be spectacular. Levinas thought that everyday courtesies that placed the other first—*après vous, monsieur*—expressed his meaning well. What I have called emotional availability (Orange, 1995) expresses this ethical attitude of proximity, of responsibility, or readiness to respond, to the other.

Substitution, unlike proximity, expresses the radical quality of Levinasian ethics. It means literally accepting the lot of the other, even

---

* As noted above, Levinas was inconsistent in his own use of upper and lower case for Other or other. He thus, perhaps deliberately, left open religious significations.
† Here we can hear the Hebrew word *dabar*. (I owe this note to historian of religion Donald A. Braue.)

death. Substitution—something we see in the subway passenger who threw himself into the path of an oncoming train to save one who had fallen onto the tracks*—never seems heroic to the one who does it: the firefighter, the doctor-without-borders, and so on. Instead, we hear, "I don't feel like a hero; anyone would do it in my place." But we wonder: Would we?

The psychoanalytic phenomenologist, I believe, has a special vocational burden, captured well in the Levinasian requirement of asymmetry discussed above. Both Buber and Binswanger believed the teacher, the therapist, and the rabbi or pastor shared an obligation to treat the student, patient, or congregant as You without expecting, or even accepting, reciprocity. Levinas in turn defined the ethical relation—the infinite responsibility for the other—as inherently asymmetrical. It is therefore no surprise that we psychoanalytic phenomenologists seem drawn to theories and clinical attitudes that emphasize our responsibility to stretch empathically, to reach for contact, to understand, just as good-enough parents do for many years, without expectation of any adequate recompense. The parent is primary support for the development of the child's personhood, and not vice versa, except in the situation of the parentified child, who grows up lacking the needed support but being required to provide it for adults. Aware of the importance of reversing such patterns, psychoanalysts and psychotherapists, I believe, work in an asymmetrical ethical relation.

So the Levinasian phenomenologist accompanies the troubled, usually traumatized, patient patiently. With good-enough attunement to emotional life, we join with the patient in the search for understanding, without too much knowing. When we guess it may support dialogic reflection, we self-disclose a little. We attempt a "minimally theoretical" psychoanalysis or other approach, working with experience-near concepts, holding our judgments and diagnostic impulses as lightly as we can. We stay close to our patients, finding our way together, we learn what we can from everyone. We seek comfort and support—always needed, sometimes desperately—primarily from fellow phenomenologists (Orange, 2009a). We face our "infinitely demanding" (Critchley, 2007) work with "radical hope" (Lear, 2006; Orange, 2008a).

Does a clinician, gripped and convinced by the Levinasian challenge, really still belong to the psychoanalytic tradition? (This question

---

* "Man Is Rescued by Stranger on Subway Tracks," *New York Times*, January 3, 2007. And Levinas: "Paradoxically, it is qua *alienus*—foreigner and other—that man is not alienated" (Levinas, 1974/1981, pp. 58–59).

may not so much concern our other humanistic therapists). The answer depends, I think, on what one considers core, and what dispensable, in the psychoanalytic tradition. If one views restraint and withholding gratification as essential; if one views the reformulation of experience as sexuality or aggression, resistance or defense; if one clings to "knowing" that all is transference as traditionally understood; if one views the psychoanalytic process as a series of enactments; if concern for the analyst's authority and authenticity are paramount; if one sees treatment as a series of negotiable dialectical opposites, then psychoanalysis and Levinasian ethics stand opposed. If on the contrary, the welcoming responses of Kohut and Winnicott, of Leo Stone and Warren Poland, appeal to us, perhaps, despite our early education, some working psychoanalysts are closet Levinasians . . . it all depends.

The implications of Levinas's radical asymmetry, "I can substitute myself for everyone, but no one can substitute himself for me" (Levinas & Nemo, 1982/1985, p. 101), seem impossible to live. How, the contemporary psychotherapist or psychoanalyst may ask, can I help the other if I allow him or her to treat me as a hostage, imperiously, thus surrendering my own agentic subjectivity? This question contains a subtle misunderstanding of Levinas's ethical humanism. The other is not being invited to mistreat me; instead, I am responsible to her need and thus the hostage of her destitution. But Levinas also saw the problem of exhaustion (burnout) that his ethics could bring, and thus characterized society, legal systems, governments as the support system—the "third party" for ethical life. In many places Levinas invoked the saying of Dostoyevsky that we are all responsible for all men before all, and I more than all the others. Although there is no escape or limit to the demand that the Face places upon me (Critchley, 2007), on the "non-interchangeable I" (Levinas & Nemo, 1982/1985, pp. 100–101), there is a "we" in the "third party" sense, and we are all responsible. Our responsibility for the other is what makes us human, and in this sense, Levinas challenges us clinicians to join him as ethical humanists.

LEVINASIAN ETHICAL HUMANISM

How is Levinasian ethics a humanism toward which psychoanalysts and other humanistically oriented psychotherapists can look for inspiration? Responding to the Heideggerian critique, Levinas wrote:

> Modern anti-humanism, which denies the primacy that the human person, free and for-itself, would have for the signification

> of Being [unwittingly] . . . clears the place for subjectivity posit-
> ing itself in abnegation [refusal of a self–centered life], in sacrifice,
> in a substitution which precedes the will. Its inspired intuition
> is to have abandoned the idea of person, goal and origin of itself,
> in which the ego is still a thing because it is still a being. Strictly
> speaking, the other is the "end"; I am a hostage, a responsibility
> and a substitution supporting the world in the passivity of assig-
> nation, even in an accusing persecution, which is indeclinable.
> Humanism has to be denounced only because it is not sufficiently
> human. (Levinas, 1974/1981, pp. 127–128)

In other words, Levinas considered himself a new kind of humanist,
unconcerned with person, freedom, and agency. He chose instead subjectivity as subjection to the other, the condition of hostage to the suffering neighbor, and utter passivity.

Against the philosophical tradition that sees the *conatus essendi*
(Spinoza) or struggle to persist in being—found also in Darwin and
Freud, of course—as essential to being, Levinas instructs us, as he
might say, "wholly otherwise." Claiming my being-in-the-world or "my
place in the sun," he often said, is "the usurpation of spaces belonging to
the other man whom I have already oppressed or starved, or driven out
into a third world; are they not acts of repulsing, excluding, stripping,
killing?" (Levinas, 1989, p. 82). Levinasian humanism is ill at ease:

> I mean to say that a truly human life cannot remain life satisfied
> in its equality to being, a life of quietude, that it is awakened by
> the other, that is to say, it is always getting sobered up, that being
> is never—contrary to what so many reassuring traditions say—its
> own reason for being, that the famous *conatus essendi* is not the
> source of all right and all meaning. (Levinas & Nemo, 1985, p. 122)

Such humanism can never remain self-satisfied, triumphant, or
comfortable. Instead it is a prophetic humanism that "comforts the
afflicted, and afflicts the comfortable." I can never say I have com-
pleted all my responsibility. I am never allowed to become compla-
cent or self-satisfied. Like the concern for the other shown by my
favorite 102-year-old who was always concerned for the safety and
well-being of others as long as she was conscious, Levinasian ethics
never ends.

Levinasian humanism does not exclude the idea of God, but in our
humanist concern for the other human being, he often said, God "comes
to mind" (Cohen, 1986, p. 25). Levinas welcomed both the Western
philosophical tradition ("Athens") and Talmudic Judaism ("Jerusalem")
as sources of his thought, but worked in each region separately, to the

extent of placing his philosophical and Judaic contributions with different publishers. Still they infuse each other. Levinas often said that he had found in Descartes the idea of infinity that he called face. Reading this thought back into his biblical studies gave him the convictions he then developed as a philosophy of infinite responsibility.

Such a humanism is not a theory, an essentialism, or a "said." It is, instead, the readiness to respond to the devastated neighbor that brings phenomenologically oriented therapists and analysts to our work, that gets us up in the morning to take on, once more, our vulnerability, our own "traumatism" as hostages in our work, recognizing the height of the other with whom we work.

FOR FURTHER READING

The interviews Philippe Nemo conducted with Levinas, *Ethics and Infinity* (1985), provide an accessible entry point. For a good secondary introduction, see *Levinas: An Introduction* (Davis, 1996). For a fascinating biography, see *Emmanuel Levinas: His Life and Legacy* (Malka, 2006).

6

HANS-GEORG GADAMER
Undergoing the Situation With the Other

The person who is understanding does not know and judge as one who stands apart and unaffected but rather he thinks along with the other from the perspective of a specific bond of belonging, as if he too were affected.

—Gadamer

There is no higher principle than this: holding oneself open to the conversation.

—Gadamer

Hans-Georg Gadamer (1900–2002) occupies the last, but not the least, of places among the philosophers we consider together as resources for contemporary humanistic psychoanalysis and psychotherapy. Like the others, he lived through the horrors of the 20th century, but unlike the others, he lived an active philosophical life into the 21st and hence realized that the work of understanding had to stretch beyond the cultural and religious heritages of Europe to engage in conversation with those we find more alien and other. At the age of 94, he delivered a lecture at Hegel Week in Bamberg, in which he claimed that dialogic understanding was the world's only hope for living together in a human way:

> Just consider the almost unbelievable miracle that the Communist revolution in China, which surely has not dealt gently with the elders, was, even with almost unlimited power, still unable to destroy the family order. So, everywhere in the world, clearly

there are individualities and customs of irreconcilable otherness. I do venture to say, however, that if we do not acquire hermeneutic virtue—that is, if we do not realize that it is essential first of all to *understand* the other person if we are ever to see whether in the end perhaps something like the solidarity of humanity as a whole may be possible, especially in relation to our living together and surviving together—if we do not do this, then we will never be able to accomplish the essential tasks of humanity, whether on a small scale or large. (2007, p. 119)

As we shall see, this passion for understanding what is other to us makes Gadamer's philosophical hermeneutics a rich resource for humanistic forms of psychotherapy such as psychoanalysis, gestalt therapy, and existential psychotherapies.

LIFE AND WORK

Like the other four philosophers discussed in this book, Gadamer suffered significant losses. Born in Marburg in 1900 to a mother who would die by the time he was 4 years old, Gadamer was raised in Breslau (now part of Poland) by his chemistry-professor father. His sister, 1 year younger, died at 5 months, and his only brother was epileptic. Of his youth in the culture of Prussian militarism, he commented later: "The way I was raised when I was a child I would wish on no one today. No child would be likely to get through it without rebellion" (Grondin, 1999/2003).

Two dominating relationships shaped his life and work: his father, who scorned his interests in the humanities and arts, and his mentor, Martin Heidegger,* who considered Gadamer not gifted enough to contribute to philosophy. (After his 100th birthday, Gadamer would still speak of how disappointing he had been to both these men.) In his middle years, he lamented that "writing, for me, has been for a long time a real torture. I always have the damned feeling that Heidegger is looking over my shoulder" (Grondin, 1999/2003, p. 12).† Nevertheless, he found his own way back into philosophy through his intensive studies of Greek and especially of Plato. His hermeneutics, the study of

---

* Hans-Georg contracted polio in his early 20s and spent his quarantine of several months reading Husserl and an early manuscript of Heidegger that affected him "like an electric shock" (Gadamer, 1985, p. 47).

† Perhaps even more important, "it is terribly painful for me to have to write. Where is my interlocutor, this silent and yet continually responding presence of the other with whom one tries to conduct a conversation, in order to carry on the conversation with oneself that is called thinking?" (Gadamer, in Grondin, 1999/2003, pp. 279-280).

meaning and interpretation, he developed into a whole philosophy of understanding emergent in dialogue.

Appalled by Heidegger's Nazi involvement, Gadamer survived the Nazi and early Communist periods in Leipzig by keeping quiet.* His political choices were complex and hard to interpret. During the Nazi period he supported and even hid Jewish friends and colleagues. But also, in desperate need of a teaching job, he twice briefly filled the positions of Jewish professors after they had been dismissed. He attended an indoctrination camp for professors before he was finally called to a permanent professorship in Leipzig, where he remained until the end of the war. Still, he never joined the Nazi party or supported the regime. After 1945, because the East Germans of the DDR (Deutsche Demokratische Republik) saw him as having undermined Nazism (Dostal, 2002), he was appointed rector (president) of the university in Leipzig, but immediately found the situation repressive. Already in 1946, he sought a position in the West, and in 1947, moved to Frankfurt.

Called to a professorial chair in Heidelberg in 1950, he taught there until his retirement in 1968, and lived there until his death in 2002. In the 1950s, he finally wrote his *Truth and Method* (1989), for which he is best known. Almost immediately, his work met a fierce challenge from German philosophy's rising star Jürgen Habermas, who thought Gadamer's hermeneutic valuing of tradition too conservative and susceptible to ideology. The debate that followed made Gadamer world-famous. After having retired, he began to study languages, and traveled and taught, especially in the United States and South America. Until his death in 2002, he engaged in his favorite form of philosophical activity, conversation (Gadamer, 2001; 2003). His influence has continued to grow in many circles, including in psychoanalysis (Orange, 2008b; Steele, 1979; Stern, 1997; Stolorow et al., 2002) and in the humanistic psychotherapies (Staemmler, 2007).

READING GADAMER

It is difficult to introduce Gadamer's texts out of context. Reading Gadamer requires an intense interest in the historical and dialogic contexts of his work, as we will see when we begin to consider the history of hermeneutics. Still, his own view is that reading is conversational, and consists of a seriously playful question-and-answer process between

---

* Some have seen him as too acquiescent, even cowardly; see Palmer (2002) and Wolin (2002). For Gadamer's own account, see Gadamer, Dutt, and Palmer (2001).

reader and text. Thus, I will make a few suggestions, hoping to draw my readers into reading Gadamer in a Gadamerian spirit.

First, as with all our philosophers, we are reading translations from languages that work quite differently from our own. When I meet someone, fluent in a first language (in German, *eine Muttersprache*), who speaks my language with some difficulty, I listen with an awareness that the words I hear resonate differently for that person, and translate only imperfectly. Speaking a second language is speaking from one world into another world within a shared world. Opportunities for misunderstanding abound. In addition, the whole style of speaking and writing may differ. German professors, for example, are infamous for the length of their sentences, which can only be understood, perhaps on the next page, when the verb appears, as Mark Twain unforgettably told us in "The Awful German Language" (1880/2003).

Gadamer, luckily for us, was sensitive to, and even theorized, problems of translation. In addition, his sentences are notably shorter than average for a German scholar. Nevertheless, reading him often sends me back to the German originals, where I find that the English words that render his meaning either do not exist or had not been chosen by the translators. The translators, for example, render his *verspielt* as "playing with life" (Gadamer, 1960/1991, p. 106). The context is a passage that contrasts a game with real risks—say, the dialogic attempt to understand—with a dilletantish approach. Now *spielen* is "to play," and Gadamer plays for pages with this word.* But *verspielen* is to gamble, to squander, to play a wrong note. We need not disparage the translators, but just to keep in mind how much we lose in translation.

There are many substantive examples, like the difference between *Erlebnis* (event experience)—"that was really an experience!"—and *Erfahrung* (accumulated learning), both usually translated "event as experience" in English. Gadamer wants to say that these inform each other and thus leads us to question the usual German usage, but the whole set of nuances gets lost in English.

More minor problems arise in the use of small words like "but," which may render *aber* (a simple but) or the untranslatable *doch*, which is a much stronger "on the contrary." In conversation it is usually said with emphasis and means "I don't agree at all!" *Doch* can be very challenging, and in nontraditional German families, may even be used by children to their parents. In translating Gadamer, the strength of his

---

* Perhaps it is no wonder that he later found himself in agreement with Wittgenstein's concept of language-games.

doch usually drops out, leaving him seeming blander in English than in his *Muttersprache*.

I bring up these problems for three reasons. First, with Gadamer, as with the other four European philosophers discussed in this book, when we struggle to understand, we could ask ourselves how much trouble they might have understanding us. We need always to be reading as if we were sitting with a patient from another culture, whose first language is not ours. Only then can we learn from the other. Second, Gadamer's own philosophy of understanding came in part from his own attempts to learn foreign languages. He came to believe that the process of understanding is generally much like learning the language of the other, and thereby working/playing toward mutual comprehension. Third, I see every clinical situation as requiring from me that I learn the patient's language (knowing that the patient has to learn mine, too). We then must both grapple moment by moment with the troubles generated by our cultural incompetence, and we must keep on trying to understand. So reading Gadamer, or any thinker we find textually difficult, is practice or training for our clinical work.

PHILOSOPHICAL HERMENEUTICS

Early hermeneutics, the study of interpretation and meaning (Hermes was the messenger-god in ancient Greece), was a set of rules and practices for interpreting texts, originally biblical texts. Friedrich Schleiermacher (1768–1834), the courageous giant of romantic hermeneutics (Schleiermacher & Frank, 1977), distinguished between a less rigorous hermeneutic practice, based on the assumption of understanding, and a more demanding life work: "There is a more rigorous practice of the art of understanding that is based on the assumption that misunderstanding occurs as a matter of course, and so understanding must be willed and sought at every point" (p. 110). In addition, Schleiermacher extended hermeneutic inquiry beyond theology to the understanding of all texts, claiming that both textual and psychological resources aided in discovering the author's intention.

Wilhelm Dilthey (1833–1911), who took the next big step in hermeneutics, was known for his distinction between the *Naturwissenschaften* (natural sciences) and the *Geisteswissenschaften* (social sciences and humanities). He contrasted their methods: the first based on mechanistic explanation; the second on hermeneutics, the attempt to understand through contextualizing. But these were not just two approaches to the same subject matter. Instead, he thought, the *Naturwissenschaften* studied causality, whereas the *Geisteswissenschaften* studied texts, cultures, and history; in short, the social sciences and humanities required hermeneutics. Hermeneutics, for Dilthey, did not involve an attempt to read the author's mind through *Einfühlung* (empathy), but rather by placing whatever needed understanding in its historical context. We make sense of the matter in question by seeing it as part of a larger whole, that is, in its historical coherence, much as a psychoanalyst tries to understand by contextualizing. Dilthey wanted to explain "how one's inner life is woven into continuity" (Gadamer, 1960/1991, p. 223). For Dilthey, "life and history have a meaning just like the letters of a word" (Gadamer, 1960/1991, p. 231, fn).

Gadamer found wanting both Schleiermacher's hermeneutics—too subjectivist with its search for the mind of the author—and Dilthey's hermeneutics: "Historical consciousness was supposed to rise above its own relativity in a way that made objectivity in the human sciences possible" (Gadamer, 1960/1991, p. 234).* In Gadamer's hands, hermeneutics became, instead, the dialogic process of understanding in which what emerges from a conversation is something unique and unexpected:

> We say that we "conduct" a conversation, but the more genuine a conversation is, the less its conduct lies within the will of either partner. Thus a genuine conversation is never the one that we wanted to conduct. Rather, it is generally more correct to say that we fall into conversation, or even that we become involved in it. The way one word follows another, with the conversation taking its own twists and reaching its own conclusion, may well be conducted in some way, but the partners conversing are far less the leaders of it than the led. No one knows in advance what will "come out" of a conversation. Understanding or its failure is like an event that happens to us. (p. 383)

Note that Gadamer refers to the interlocutors in a dialogue as "partners" or as "we," not as individuals. For him, the concept of individuality seemed to represent an individualistic reversion to romantic hermeneutics, with its attempts to enter the mind of the author. "We do not try to transpose ourselves into the author's mind but . . . . we try to transpose ourselves into the perspective within which he has formed his views . . . we try to understand how what he is saying could be right" (p. 292). Understanding, he wrote, "is not based on transposing oneself into another person. . . . To understand what a person says is . . . to come to an understanding about the subject matter, not to get inside another person and relive his experiences" (p. 383). In a genuine dialogue, people

---

* Like Merleau-Ponty and Wittgenstein, Gadamer wrote one big book, *Truth and Method* (1960/1991).

do attempt to convince each other, but they always also listen with the expectation that the other can teach them something. Under this condition, understanding can emerge in the play of conversation. Again,

> Hermeneutics is *die Kunst der Verstaendigung*—the art of reaching an understanding—of something or with someone . . . . This "coming to an understanding" of our practical situations and what we must do in them is not monological; rather, it has the character of a conversation. We are dealing with each other. Our human form of life has an "I and thou" character and an "I and we" character, and also a "we and we" character. In our practical affairs we depend on our ability to arrive at an understanding. And reaching an understanding happens in conversation, in a dialogue. (Gadamer, 2001, p. 79)

The practice of conversation, for Gadamer, had the kind of priority that it had held for Socrates (Gadamer, 1960/1991, pp. 361–362), that dialogic inclusion had for Buber, that the neighbor's need had for Levinas, and that conversation holds for humanistic psychoanalysis and psychotherapies. But conversation, or dialogue, has a double function. Though oriented toward increased understanding (*Verständigung*), its process disquiets (Davey, 2006), disturbs, and unsettles our previous points of view and settled convictions.

HERMENEUTIC PRACTICE AS CRITIQUE

The philosophical hermeneutics of Hans-Georg Gadamer can serve, I believe, a double function for psychoanalysis and other humanistic forms of psychotherapy: critical and constructive. To theorists of justice ethics like Habermas,* the critical aspects of Gadamer's work have often seemed invisible; to a post-Freudian psychoanalyst, on the other hand, philosophical hermeneutics constitutes a large and radical critique of the ideology of traditional theory and practice. Critical features include (a) the Gadamerian refusal of all forms of authoritarian communication (while recognizing the legitimate authority of tradition); (b) an unmasking of the pretensions of interpretive expertise, discarding notions of empathy as reading the mind of the author or patient; (c) a theory of emergent and self-correcting understanding. These forms of critique, useful for psychoanalytic thinking, show that Gadamer's philosophy contains important critical and self-questioning elements, and that it can thus withstand the

---

* For Habermas, conversation shaped by tradition offered insufficient guarantees against repetition of the horrors ideology had created in the 20th century. See Warnke (1987).

"too conservative" challenge (Warnke, 1987). Let us consider these critical features in turn.

Psychoanalysis, first, especially as practiced in North America (Hale, 1995) though not only here,* absorbed a strongly authoritarian flavor from its identification with the medical profession.† The doctor or psychoanalyst is the one who knows, and whose orders must be obeyed. Like the "noncompliant" medical patient, the "resistant" psychoanalytic or psychotherapeutic patient may be reluctant to lie on the couch, to follow the fundamental rule (say *everything* that comes to mind), and to accept the withholding of all personal engagement with the analyst (do not gratify the instinctual wishes). Similarly, we may attribute "negative therapeutic reactions," "borderline personality" (Brandchaft & Stolorow, 1990), or "inauthenticity" to a patient who protests the confrontational style of some contemporary psychoanalysis or of classical gestalt therapy. This patient needs to be confronted with the aggressive or transgressive contents of his or her unconscious mind.

Recently, however, several influences have converged to support the emergence of a cluster of relational forms of psychoanalysis and psychotherapy, particularly in North America: the study of infant research and attachment theories; dissatisfaction with the narrow range of patients treatable in the prescribed ways; an embracing of philosophical pragmatism (Sullivan, 1953, p. 309); an engagement with European phenomenology; and, increasingly, an interest in theories of complex self-organizing systems. To these influences, I would add a quiet—though nonetheless powerful—sensibility derived from Gadamer's philosophical hermeneutics, whose practice embodies the refusal of authoritarian theory and forms of relatedness, and embraces conversation (*Gespräch*).

A second though crucially related aspect of critique is the Gadamerian undoing of the interpretive expert-authority who uncovers the mental contents and motivations of the author or patient. In psychoanalysis—including some contemporary forms—many have thought it possible and desirable *to read the patient's mind* by means of empathy (*Einfühlung*). Gadamer would have none of this. But the idea that we can know what the other would think and desire without actual conversation survives, I think, in some forms of Kantian-inspired justice ethics, where we are asked to imagine ourselves into the "initial situation" (Rawls, 1971) or

---

* Both the Kleinian tradition, practiced especially in Europe and Latin America, and the Lacanian, practiced mainly in France, share this tone. See Etchegoyen (1991).

† It might have been otherwise. Freud studied five terms with proto-phenomenologist Franz Brentano and wanted, as a young man, to be a professor of philosophy (Herzog, 1988).

into the ideal emancipatory situation (Habermas, 1981/1984). Whether considering ethical political arrangements in society or attempting to understand the other therapeutically, a Gadamerian critique occurs in an actual and historically situated engagement with the other to whom we listen and with whom we converse. What we hear will often constitute a challenge to, or critique of, our preconceived ideas. Every time a patient says to me, "No, that's not exactly what I meant. It's more like this . . .," critique is already in play.

A third form of Gadamerian critique is the theory of truth emergent from the conversational interplay: As noted above, "a genuine conversation is never the one that we wanted to conduct. Rather, it is generally more correct to say that we fall into conversation, or even that we become involved in it" (Gadamer, 1960/1991, p. 383). This process has a self-correcting quality reminiscent of Peirce's (1960) account of self-correcting inquiry within a community of scholars (Vol. 5, p. 189). The critical function is, I think, importantly built into Gadamer's idea of understanding emergent in dialogue. His *Horizontverschmelzung* (fusion of horizons) occurs only if both interlocutors are willing to risk their prejudices, organizing principles (Stolorow et al., 1987), emotional convictions (Orange, 1995), or as Gadamer himself called them, our "binding expectations." Together we can find a provisional understanding, at least a moment in which our perspectives on the matter under discussion (*die Sache*) overlap. Such unstable and open moments of *Horizontverschmelzung* serve as place markers for continued dialogue. This hermeneutics of trust, as opposed to the "hermeneutics of suspicion" Ricoeur (1970) attributed to Marx and to Freud, requires a nonauthoritarian and nonideological psychoanalysis and psychotherapy, prepared to welcome the other into conversation.

It could be argued that every time we begin a conversation, there is an implicit critique of what both parties have previously taken for granted. Nothing—whether ideology or emotional conviction—survives interpretive dialogue intact. This is especially evident in clinical work, where an ongoing inquiry into previously held "facts" or "emotional truths" creates disruption. Modest and patient work in a hermeneutic spirit can, I believe, transform devastated lifeworlds into possibilities for shared understanding. Reciprocally, such hermeneutically informed psychoanalytic work constitutes some evidence for the critical possibilities within Gadamer's philosophical hermeneutics. A psychoanalytic hermeneut, always intent on learning from the other, lives emancipatory critique: "The task of bringing people to a self-understanding of themselves may help us to gain our freedom in relation to everything that has taken us in unquestioningly" (Gadamer, 1982, pp. 149–150).

CONSTRUCTIVE RESOURCES FOR CLINICAL WORK

In addition, Gadamerian hermeneutics constitutes an important intellectual and inspirational resource for those forms of psychoanalysis that survive the critique outlined above. This hermeneutics teaches the clinician (a) to regard the patient in the dialogic situation as an important source of truth, (b) to take developmental and cultural contexts seriously, and (c) to adapt an attitude of serious play that puts the clinician's emotional life and convictions at risk for the sake of the possible understanding. Why does this inspiration matter? Or is critique enough? Important as they are, formal theories of justice like those of Habermas and Rawls need to be balanced by what Stanley Cavell (1990) calls "perfectionist" ethics, that is, by some account of what kind of human life with each other is possible and good. Psychoanalytic and psychotherapeutic work relies for their legitimacy and inspiration, at least implicitly, on such accounts of the human good. Not only the *Ich-Du* of Martin Buber (1923/1970) and the face of the Other (*Autrui*) of Emmanuel Levinas (1961/1969), but also the *Verstaendigung* philosophy of Hans-Georg Gadamer can provide us this inspiration.

A hermeneutic *attitude* offers a rich resource for contemporary psychotherapeutic and psychoanalytic theory and practice. First, Gadamer often recommended that we approach every conversation hoping and expecting to learn something from our interlocutor. Such an attitude places the other, if not above me (Levinas, 1961/1969), at least as my equal in the search for truth and understanding. Though some may say that Gadamer underestimated power relations in his dialogic hermeneutics, it seems to me that he precisely refused to see all human relatedness in terms of domination and submission. Not that interlocutors do not attempt to convince each other, but each also stays available to *be convinced*, at least in part, by the other. In a dialogic psychoanalysis or psychotherapy, neither partner emerges unchanged. Neither is a "somebody" whose status or rank is created by "nobodying" the other (Fuller, 2006).

A second helpful aspect is Gadamer's insistence that all understanding is historically situated, or as we clinicians might say, developmentally conditioned. For him, as for the younger Heidegger, temporality and embeddedness in history and culture are foregrounded and are inescapable. Heidegger's groundbreaking work, *Sein und Zeit* (*Being and Time*, 1962), emerged from his attempt to rearticulate Aristotle's concretely situated *phronesis* (practical wisdom) within the inescapable temporal situatedness of human being (Dasein). It would be almost correct to say that the younger Heidegger conceived being *as* temporality, to be is to be in time (*zeitlich*).

Similarly, Gadamer's (1980) dialogic philosophy has been developed from a very long conversation with the Greeks, especially with Plato. For Gadamer, tradition is the condition for the possibility of understanding or interpreting anything, just as, for most psychoanalysts, developmental history—explicitly spoken or not—is indispensable for understanding, restoration, and development. To understand a text or a person, hermeneuts and psychoanalysts agree, is to understand how that text or person—whether patient or therapist—emerged within living contexts, cultures, or traditions. Such rootedness is primordial and inevitable. As the hermeneutic dialogue always brings into play the background of prejudice and tradition that all participants bring to the conversation, Gadamer (1976) saw this background as the condition for the possibility of understanding anything:

> It is not so much our judgments as it is our prejudices that constitute our being . . . the concept of prejudice did not originally have the meaning we have attached to it. Prejudices are not necessarily unjustified and erroneous, so that they inevitably distort the truth. In fact the historicity of our existence entails that prejudices, in the literal sense of the word, constitute the initial directedness of our whole ability to experience. Prejudices are biases of our openness to the world. They are simply conditions whereby we experience something—whereby what we encounter says something to us. This formulation certainly does not mean that we are enclosed within a wall of prejudices and only let through narrow portals those things that can produce a pass that says, "nothing new will be said here." Instead we welcome just that guest who promises something new to our curiosity. (p. 9)

We are always embedded in history, in *wirkungsgeschichtliches Bewusstsein* (historically effective/effected consciousness),* in temporality and relatedness. We can understand only from within the interplay of traditions or contexts from which we cannot entirely extricate ourselves.

Working in New York, I often encounter patients whose sense of loss and sorrow, medically diagnosed as "clinical depression," seems to exceed whatever account the person can give of the sorrow's origin. Not until I begin to wonder out loud about what losses have shadowed the life of these patients' families do I hear about the losses of whole

---

* Jean Grondin (2003) translates *wirkungsgeschichtliches Bewusstsein* as "a consciousness of being affected by history" (p. 8).

families to the Shoah or about the concentration camp survivors. Each suffering person suffers in multiple contexts that give the current trouble layers of meaning—sedimentation for Merleau-Ponty, memory for Levinas, *wirkungsgeschichtliches Bewusstsein* for Gadamer.

Suppose, for example, that a therapeutic hermeneut meets a patient who has been unable to recover from the loss of a girlfriend 2 years earlier. A talented young attorney, indeed a rising star who has had, to all appearances, every advantage in parental support and education, he cannot understand his continuing sorrow and depression. An additional difficulty was his tendency to fall into profound and depressive states of shame and self-hatred at the smallest hint or threat of failure or shortcoming in work or friendships. The significant circumstances, he thinks, are the suddenness and unexplained nature of the breakup, and the continued necessity of seeing the lost other at work every day. After some time exploring the patient's own interpretations of his trouble, his therapist asked him if there was a history of loss in his family. Not surprisingly, there had been deaths of three grandparents within the past 3 years. Two of these grandparents had lived with the patient's family for extended periods of time. The analyst, loss-sensitive for her own reasons and inclined to feel losses as humiliating rejections, then asked if there might be more to tell about these grandparents. It turned out that all four grandparents were Shoah survivors, who had either fled, or nearly died in concentration camps. They had all been extremely reluctant to speak of their experiences, so that the culture of the extended family, as well as of the beloved home, included (a) a strong injunction not to speak of any sorrows; (b) a sense that anyone might be violently taken away at any time; and (c) a sense, common in families who have suffered devastating losses, that the children must be more than perfect to compensate for unspeakable horrors and losses.

Such nondramatic, hermeneutically sensitive, dialogic work has given this patient a sense of the shape of his experiential world, with its haunted places and impending horrors. Of course, we have only just begun.

A hermeneutic sensibility contributes to clinical thinking, thirdly, in what today we might call a systems view. Mitchell (1988) and many other relational psychoanalysts insist that the analyst is never separate from the reality under consideration, that is, the patient's trouble. Not only do we always understand through our own situated emotional history and our theories, but also our situated engagement shapes and participates in this "reality under consideration," that is, the patient's trouble. The trouble immediately becomes not only your trouble or my trouble (never absent from the processes of understanding) but also *our* trouble. A hermeneutic approach to understanding thus fits perfectly with most relational approaches to psychoanalysis, including intersubjective systems work (Atwood & Stolorow, 1984; Orange et al., 1997; Stolorow et al., 2002).

There are additional contributions. Hermeneutics fits easily with a descriptive phenomenology in psychoanalysis that avoids diagnostic labeling and reductionistic categories. Its attention to fore-understanding or, preconceptions—for Gadamer, prejudices—keeps us close to our patient's experience. Before we call the patient borderline, manipulative, sadistic, or projectively identifying, we can ask ourselves why we need to use such labels, and attempt to understand with the patient whatever experience is in question—yours, mine, and ours—past, present, and future. In a fallibilistic spirit, we may be slow to foreclose possibilities of understanding; ready to hold our own perceptions, opinions, and theoretical language lightly; and prepared to allow the inquiry to rest when the patient says the understanding is good enough for now. In other words, we work as partners in the search for understanding, but not as the authority who says that bedrock (Freudian/Kleinian drives, the patient's aggression, or *the* meaning of a "delusion" or a symptom or a dream) has been reached. We hermeneuts, acknowledging our own understanding as severely limited (Davey, 2006), refuse to insist on our own point of view. "OK," we respond to the patient who dissents, "tell me how it seems to you."

Another advantage of a hermeneutic sensibility in psychotherapeutic work, and one that often provides a useful focus, is the hermeneutic advice to take what is most difficult to understand—in a dream, in a patient's self-description or story, in a particular patient-analyst interaction—as the centerpiece of inquiry. Understanding this focus can often help us to understand other parts of the picture. What emerges from such a shared conversation may be a relatively clear, though previously perhaps unsuspected, articulation of the most basic emotional convictions (in intersubjective systems theory called "organizing principles," in Gadamer, the "binding expectations" (Grondin, 1999/2003) that structure a person's psychological world, or lifeworld*).

An undramatic patient, despite apparent professional and social success, feels depressed and fearfully alone, at the moments of greatest success. The other pieces of the life story seem to interpret themselves rather easily—perhaps too easily. This puzzling disparity, though

---

* This process follows from awareness of the long-recognized "hermeneutic circle" (Schleiermacher, 1998), in which the whole can be understood only through the parts, and the parts through the whole. Gadamer, seeing that the circle need not be vicious, reinterpreted it as consisting of reader and author, or more generally as partners in dialogue who mutually require each other.

less frequently experienced than the more daily troubles, is the hardest for us to understand. So, we decide together to make this puzzle the center of our inquiry. After much musing together, much playing with possibly related factors, many discarded hypotheses, we may find a strong shared sense that this patient has long deeply felt that getting public attention would mean losing whatever attachments were most important to her, and that thus she would be completely, desperately, and irredeemably alone. Or perhaps if she ever outshone the family's designated star or genius, that is, if she emerged momentarily from her assigned Cinderella role, she would lose whatever relational world she had. Or perhaps we find that, having grown up with less intelligent or less successful parents, this person has always felt any success as a sign that she is not really even human, or doesn't belong to these people, or anywhere. And so on. The hermeneutic task is to search together, taking as the central question whatever is most puzzling or surprising, for an understanding that allows us to then organize our understanding of everything else that we consider together (working through). We do not claim that that the experiential world we (analyst and patient) seek to understand is fully created by us, nor that it fully preexists (a "preexisting condition") our attempt to understand it. Usually, in my experience, the sense is more of discovery of the unexpected (aha, so that was/is the trouble!), more a gestalt shift, than of the satisfaction one takes in an entirely new creation.† "Every experience worthy of the name thwarts an expectation" (Gadamer, 1960/1991, p. 356).*

This last aspect—that Gestalt shift that Gadamer calls a fusion of horizons—addresses the problem of the therapeutic efficacy of psychoanalysis and psychotherapy and provides an alternative to the currently popular constructivist "postmodernism" (Hoffman, 2001). As we suggested in a recent work on a horizonal metaphor for unconsciousness (Stolorow et al., 2002), the relational experience of the recontextualization and reorganization of emotional experience (the finding together in the context of emotional engagement, often an experience of good-enough attachment, of unsuspected emotional organizing convictions), can become profoundly healing and open new lifeworld possibilities. Understanding emerges from the dialogic world within which we play with possible meanings ("truth-as-possible-understanding," Frank, 1992) while the process itself both de-rigidifies overly structured expectancies—often

---

* See also Buber on surprise, Chapter 2.

† In fact, this sense probably in part explains my preference for hermeneutics over constructivist psychoanalysis. See Orange (2009c), where I have developed this contrast at greater length.

traumatically generated—and creates space for emergent possibility. Thus, the daily experience of psychoanalytic work—the struggles to understand, the misunderstandings necessary to understanding, the extension of change beyond the areas explicitly discussed in analysis or therapy—all make sense in hermeneutic terms.

True, the process of understanding creates, but not *ex nihilo*. Understanding differs from the processes of construction and deconstruction. As the French tradition has clearly seen, what is constructed can always be deconstructed, seen as arbitrary or as less than inevitable. And yes, the processes of understanding in psychoanalysis commonly lead us to see as questionable what we had always regarded as certain and internal truths—for example, our own worthlessness or unimportance to others. Not only these background emotional convictions, but also the meanings we "discover" together, could in principle be otherwise. Nevertheless, the ideas of understanding and interpretation suggest that there is something to be understood, and that this something makes its own claims on us who seek to understand. Noticing and acknowledging our assumptions within the therapeutic conversation is the beginning of change.

A patient's serious suicide attempt, together with his view that it was a desperate attempt to call his parents' attention to the impact of 4 years of abuse by the local priest, cries out for understanding within some community and for an understanding witness that allows its meanings to emerge in dialogue. When he finally found enough support to tell them, the parents' only words were, "We don't believe you." The suicide attempt followed. We could say that this family had co-constructed a system in which it seemed unsafe to the patient to ask for protection. Or we could say that (later) analysis had constructed this whole story, and we would in one sense not be wrong. But such construction-talk, in my view, tends to distance clinicians from the outrages our patients have suffered and thus protects us from feeling with them. We become a milder version of the invalidating parents in this story, and our distancing attitude may retraumatize the patient.

Similarly, George Atwood tells a story from his years of inpatient work with those diagnosed as schizophrenic. The patient and her therapist were walking on the hospital grounds one day when she pointed out that behind a nearby tree, there lurked a ghost (Orange, 2009c). In the clinical case conference, he was told that he should take the patient over to the tree, walk her around it, and say, "Look, no ghost!" Instead, he had looked thoughtfully at the patient and said, "I believe in ghosts," and proceeded to engage her in a conversation about this particular ghost and its place in her world and in the world they inhabited together. Again, "We do not try to transpose ourselves into the author's mind but . . . we try to transpose ourselves into the perspective within which he has formed his views . . . we try to understand how what he is saying could be right" (Gadamer, 1960/1991, p. 292).

Thus, a hermeneutic practice and attitude, instead, is to take what my patient says seriously (not necessarily literally) and to try to make sense of it together. If, instead, I meet my patient's terror and confusion with a deconstructive distancing* attitude, it seems to me, I may have abandoned my patient. I have then, constructivist style (Hacking, 1999), preferred what Ricoeur (1970) called the "hermeneutics of suspicion," and of which Gadamer would have no part. To me it seems that to choose to undergo-the-situation with the patient in the search for understanding helps to sustain compassionate clinical work.

UNDERSTANDING AND COMPASSION

I think a therapeutic practice that is complexity-and-context-sensitive will be characterized by compassion,[†] a sensibility that for me expresses itself best in hermeneutic terms. *Compassion,* a word that appears rarely in psychoanalytic literature,[‡] is a word with resonances that come from its use in many discourses or language-games. In everyday English, compassion often connotes pity or sympathy and thus, for psychoanalysts, could further connote the being-nice-to-patients often disparagingly attributed to self psychology. For relational psychoanalysis, however, including intersubjective systems theory and some contemporary versions of self psychology, compassion could belong in respectable theoretical and clinical discourse. Most analysts continue to refer to analysands as patients (*patior,* to suffer, undergo). A patient is one who suffers, one who bears what feels unbearable. Compassion (*compatior*), then, is etymologically, a suffering-with, a bearing together.[§]

---

* We have seen that distance can be respectful (Buber), part of ethical proximity (Levinas), or rejecting of our common humanity (Gadamer). Context matters, as Wittgenstein would have shown us.
† This section draws on Orange (2006).
‡ Heinz Kohut was concerned carefully to distinguish empathy from compassion, noting that empathic modes of perception could be used cruelly. In his last work (Kohut, Goldberg, & Stepansky, 1984) however, he began to ask why feelings of compassion seemed to expand his capacity for empathy. I tend to think of empathy as a larger capacity to understand another emotional experience from within an intersubjective field. Compassion, in my view, is that part of empathy that makes us willing and able to descend into and to explore the Dantean realms of suffering with the other.
§ In apparent contrast, Levinas, as we have seen, described our response to the other's suffering as radically asymmetrical, but I think the spirit here is not so different.

Compassion is not technique, and even less a rule of technique; instead it is both process and attitude. As process, compassion is roughly equivalent to emotional understanding (Orange, 1995), the dialogic process of undergoing the situation with the other (Gadamer, 1960/1991), and coming-to-an-understanding (*Verständigung*). We make sense together (Buirski & Haglund, 2001) of the patient's emotional predicament within the relational system that we experience together, and gradually this shared world changes. A compassionate attitude, which may not always seem gentle or nice—indeed it may occasionally challenge or contradict or introduce alternative perspectives—enables hitherto unknown and impossible forms of experiencing. Likewise, a listening hermeneut may try energetically to convince the interlocutor (Gadamer, 2003). But implicit and explicit forms of participation in the patient's suffering create a world of compassion that brings new experiential possibilities. This hermeneutic participation, however, is a way of *being*-with, not a formula or technique (Orange et al., 1997) for *doing* clinical work. Where there was indifference, humiliation, rejection, shattering loss, and the like, compassionate therapeutic understanding does not simply replace or heal by intentionally providing new experience. Instead, treating a person as endlessly worth understanding, deeming his or her suffering as worth feeling together, an attitude of compassion implicitly affirms the human worth of the patient. The psychoanalytic or psychotherapeutic relationship can accord to the patient, often for the first time, the dignity of being treated as the subject of one's own experience.

Psychoanalytic and psychotherapeutic hermeneuts see many patients who, because of their previous experience in life and in treatment, come to us expecting to be classified, judged, treated with rigidity, or exploited. If, however, the analyst or therapist is not too intent on naming pathologies and defenses, with deconstructing, or with being right, but instead relentlessly seeks to understand and accompany the sufferer, a virtual interpretive system emerges. For me, close and compassionate listening is itself an important form of interpretation, dissolving the interpretation/gratification duality,* and fully deserves to be considered psychoanalytic. It says to the other: "You are worth hearing and understanding." This listening includes attention to the ways the patient's experiential world has created suffering for the patient as

---

* Unlike gestalt therapists, enjoined to "never interpret," psychoanalysts have been taught "never gratify." We learned that kindness might interfere with the essential psychoanalytic work of interpreting the contents of the unconscious.

well as for others in the patient's life. Without leaving the patient's side or becoming judgmental, we can understand how one could come to be so hurtful to oneself and to others. We can understand the simultaneous two-sided experience—so often dissociated—of being both hurt and hurtful. Recognizing context and complexity prevents reduction and judgmental attitudes, and enables compassionate understanding.

Often we hermeneut clinicians bear witness to outrageous forms of mistreatment, whether abuse of children or adults, from bullying through torture (Orange, 1995). But very often simple accompanying—"undergoing the situation"—that some would contrast with proper "analytic" work and might disparage as "supportive" psychotherapy becomes our central task. Whether my patient suffers from an incurable, painful, debilitating disease or from terminal cancer, or has lost a family member in the World Trade Center, I must not look for ways to see my patients as constructing or even contributing to their suffering and thus join those who tell them just to accept it or get over it. Often there is no way to fix the situation or to "cure" the patients, so I must accept my own powerlessness to help. I must simply stay close to their experience, sorrowing and grieving and raging with my patients, even if this means that my practice feels very heavy to me. Even when—and it always is—the story is very complex, a willingness to walk together into the deepest circles of the patient's experiential hell* characterizes the *attitude* of compassion or emotional availability (Orange, 1995) that I believe the process of clinical understanding requires. This psychoanalytic compassion, I repeat for emphasis, is not reducible to moral masochism on the part of the analyst, nor is it to be contrasted with properly psychoanalytic work, too often seen as explicitly interpretive, or as confronting aggression. It is, instead, an implicitly interpretive process of giving lived meaning and dignity to a shattered person's life by enabling integration of the pain and loss as opposed to dissociation or fragmentation. A compassionate attitude says to every patient: your suffering is human suffering, and when the bell tolls for you, it also tolls for me (Orange, 2006, 2009a).

Thus I believe that a dialogic hermeneutics of compassion encourages the vocational sense that most psychoanalysts and humanistically oriented psychotherapists† bring to their thinking and practice. Hermeneutics preserves the psychoanalytic emphasis on interpretation and the relational emphasis on engaged understanding. At the

---

* Virgil was Dante's guide (Dante, trans. 1994).
† A hermeneutic sensibility characterizes much contemporary thinking in Gestalt therapy. Frank-M. Staemmler (2009), for example, opposes rigid use of techniques in favor of a Gadamerian search for understanding in dialogue.

same time, as practical wisdom or phronesis—unlike technique—
it keeps us humble and flexible. By *phronesis*, both Aristotle and
Gadamer meant a kind of learned practical wisdom (Dreyfus, 2008)
typical of the humanistic ideal of the wise person. In contrast with
episteme (theoretical knowing) and *techne* (knowing how to make
something that needs to be done to specifications), *phronesis* is the
capacity to find the right thing to do in a situation. Ethics and politics, Aristotle thought, and all forms of understanding between persons, texts, and works of art, Gadamer thought, needed this situated
kind of knowing. This kind of knowing remains, by its nature, fallible
and open-ended. To my mind, *phronesis* includes, for us clinicians, a
graceful kind of humility.

GADAMER'S HERMENEUTIC HUMANISM

In the introduction we noted that Heidegger's "Letter on Humanism"
created a challenge for those he influenced. How could we accept his
account of human being as worlded and, bypassing his critique, call
ourselves humanists? Many of us simply refuse to allow him to limit
our use of words that have meanings in the worlds that are ours. But
Hans-Georg Gadamer, with his "damned feeling" noted above, faced a
more complex task. Having recognized the force of Heidegger's rejection of humanism, he had to show why his philosophical hermeneutics
belonged squarely in the humanistic tradition. In the words of his student and later biographer Jean Grondin, "Gadamer is a humanist and
Heidegger isn't" (Gadamer & Hahn, 1997, p. 157). In Grondin's view, this
divergence is exactly where Gadamer finished being a Heideggerian.
How so?

First of all, Gadamer belonged to, and profoundly valued, the traditional studies or literature, history, and the arts that in English we call
"the humanities" (in the German *Gymnasium*, or academically oriented
secondary school, these studies constitute "*Germanistik*"). Although
his conception of humanity and of the humanities became ever more
inclusive, his world was the humanistic heritage—the university world
of the humanities, the world he had to protect from his scientist-father's
scorn. How ironic that he had to protect it from Heidegger as well.

Second, for Gadamer, hermeneutics itself was always a human, not a
technical, pursuit. The reading of a text, the appreciation of art, the serious and playful attempt to understand another—all these were dialogic
for him, modes of conversation. Conversation, for him, was exactly what
made us human. He invoked the German tradition of *Bildung*, or cultural education, to teach us that all interpretation develops within the

humanistic world (Davey, 2006). "What distinguishes our humanity is not any rational capacity that would catapult us into a divine world of pure ideas, but rather only the ability to go beyond our particularity, to take into account the heritage that can help us grow above our limited selves" (Gadamer & Hahn, 1997, p. 164). Without explicit theological reference or Heideggerian hints, Gadamer's dialogue is always between mortal, fallible, and limited human beings. Wisdom is difficult, human, and primarily practical (*phronesis*).

Third, and here is where his humanism meets that of Buber and of Levinas, Gadamer's hermeneutics of understanding was not methodic, as he understood earlier hermeneutics to have been,* but rather the pursuit of truth by the conversation of question and answer. The Gadamerian hermeneut does not enter the mind of the other, but instead asks what question the interlocutor attempts to answer by saying what she or he says. The hermeneutic circle in Gadamer's hands becomes the mutual interplay of learning from each other in coming to an understanding. So "humanistic" describes Gadamer, the philosopher of coming-to-an-understanding (*Verständigung*). As for Levinas, the face of the other places an infinite responsibility on me, so, for Gadamer, the voice of the other (Risser, 1997) is an endless call to the hermeneut: Never give up the search for mutual understanding. "A conversation," he said, "is always a kind of living together and as such it has its incontestable and unreachable priority" (Gadamer & Hahn, 1997, pp. 403–404).

FOR FURTHER READING

A good entry for Gadamer is to read him in the conversations he loved: *Gadamer in Conversation: Reflections and Commentary* (Gadamer, 2001). For a secondary introduction, see *Gadamer: A Guide for the Perplexed* (Lawn, 2006).

---

* Arguably, in Schleiermacher's case, this was a misunderstanding (Schleiermacher, 1977).

AFTERWORD

This book surprised me. My initial intention to create a bridge between my philosophical and my clinical lives by linking them for my colleagues in psychoanalysis and in the humanistic psychotherapies remained intact. What I did not expect was the extent to which the ethical aspects of this bridge would come into focus. Whether or not these philosophers lived in the "ivory tower," each lived and expressed a profound concern for ethics, for the good beyond being. Explaining their philosophies for my clinician colleagues, I found myself more and more absorbed in and convinced by their ethical questions, as my text probably shows.

I had always seen psychoanalytic and psychotherapeutic work as a profession in the vocational sense (not just *Beruf* or job, but *Berufung* or vocation). Working with these philosophers gave me a sense that it is no wonder that we feel so drained by our work, but that it is nevertheless profoundly and humanly right that we should do it. Heeding Wittgenstein's admonition to be silent when there are no words, but also needing to speak the words of hospitality and compassion, I end by saying thank you again to the philosophers, Socratics all, who have changed me.

GLOSSARY

Alterity: In contemporary philosophy, the quality of being other than, and other to, the speaker.

Ambiguity/Ambiguous: Capable of various meanings. In Merleau-Ponty, a positive quality of all experience.

Attachment theory: Pioneered by John Bowlby, Mary Salter Ainsworth, and Mary Main, the view that experiences of attachment, separation, and loss are central to psychological development.

Autrui: In Levinas, "the other," the irreducible and irreplaceable other whose claim on me is infinite and to whom I am infinitely responsible.

Befindlichkeit: In Heidegger, sense or mood of how one finds oneself in one's world. Sometimes translated as "affectivity."

Being-in-the-world: Heidegger's expression, replacing the isolated mind of modern philosophy, for our inextricable rootedness in our surroundings.

Body-subject: In Merleau-Ponty, key to overcoming body-mind dualism. Body as experiencer and experienced.

Categorical imperative: In Kant, the moral requirement to act in such a way that we could wish that everyone would do the same. In another Kantian formulation, the requirement to treat others as ends in themselves, never as means only.

Cause: In modern philosophy, equivalent to Aristotle's efficient cause, what makes something happen or change.

Chiasm (ki-asm): In Merleau-Ponty's last work, the intricate intertwining of the visible (embodiment) and the invisible (spirit).

Cogito: "I think, therefore I am." In Descartes, the foundational conviction that survived his methodical doubt.

Cognitive science: A contemporary cluster of studies, including and sometimes replacing philosophy of mind, epistemology, artificial intelligence, and cognitive neuroscience. Its central question is the nature of consciousness.

Confirmation (*Bestätigung*): In Buber, recognition of the other's potentiality. Making the other present as that unique person. Similar to Kohut's self-consolidation through the relation to the other.

Construction: Creation of concepts or meanings. Usually used to contrast with meanings or essences thought to inhere in things, ready to be discovered.

Constructivism: A view, typical of postmodernism, that all meanings are constructed or made, as opposed to given. See also *postmodernism* and *deconstruction*.

Contact: In gestalt therapy, and in Buber, direct personal meeting within the interhuman.

Deconstruction: In Derrida and other postmodernists, the unmasking of concepts—which are regarded as constructed—to see what assumptions they systematically hide from view.

Determinism: The view that things must be as they are, that efficient causality explains everything, and that freedom is an illusion.

Dialectic: In Plato, the process of dialogue. In Hegel and in most later thinkers, the generation of opposites from each other, to be understood more fully as parts of a larger whole.

Dogmatism: Treating opinions as beyond discussion.

Dualism: A theory, formal or informal, that organizes the world around perceived oppositions, and treats these oppositions as substantial. The classical example is Descartes, whose mind-body, subject-object, reason-emotion dualisms have shaped Western philosophy since the early 17th century.

Emanation: In Plotinus, the emergence of the world from the divine.

Embodiment: In Merleau-Ponty's response to dualism, our mode of perceptual being in the world, as body-subject.

Empiricism: The view that sense experience, experimental results, or "data points" are the only reliable source of knowledge. It denies that we have innate ideas, or can depend on reason alone for knowledge.

Epistemology: In philosophy generally, the theory of knowledge, what it is, and what justifies our claims to have it.

Essence: That which makes something what it is and not something else. Contrasts with nonessential or accidental qualities.

Ethics: Theories of justice, of the good human life. In Levinas, the responsibility to the neighbor that precedes all such theories.

Existentialism: The philosophies of existence and freedom prevalent in the 1950s and 1960s. Origins in Kierkegaard and Nietzsche, flowering in France with Sartre, de Beauvoir, and Camus.

Fallibilism: The pragmatists' view that all knowledge is prone to incompleteness and mistakes and is therefore a work in progress. Encourages holding theory lightly.

Family resemblance: In Wittgenstein, the view that what words or things have in common is not an identical essence but rather overlapping commonalities, as in a family.

Flesh (*le chair*): In Merleau-Ponty's last work, the whole of the human, interwoven and embodied in the world.

Gestalt psychology: In the Berlin school of the 1930s, the psychological whole differs from the sum of its parts, as in a constellation. Especially refers to perception. This school influenced Merleau-Ponty, Gadamer, and Wittgenstein.

Gestalt therapy: A school of humanistic psychotherapy, influenced by the gestalt psychologists, that emphasizes not only the emergence of figure from ground, but Buber's concepts of contact, inclusion, and confirmation.

Hermeneutics: The study of interpretation, originally biblical interpretation; gradually extended from textual study to become, for Gadamer, the attempt to reach understanding with others in dialogue.

Horizon: In Heidegger and others, the edges of the experiential world, or meaning-context, formed by the position into which we have been thrown, and felt in the mode of *Befindlichkeit* (see above). The limits of what we can understand from where we are.

Idealism: The philosophical view, opposed to materialism and dualism, that only ideas are fully real.

Implicit: Contained within what has been said, nonexplicit. In contemporary cognitive science and psychoanalysis, a realm of experience and meaning that precedes or escapes verbal expression.

Inclusion (*Umfassung*): In Buber, meeting the other as a fellow human within the human community. Also connotes "embrace."

Induction: Reasoning from particulars to the general rule.

Intentionality: In Brentano and in phenomenology, the aboutness of all mental life: In thinking, we think something; in desiring, we desire something, and so on.

Intersubjectivity: In Husserl, and in later phenomenologists, the betweenness of psychological experience. For psychoanalytic intersubjectivists influenced by Hegel, the paradigm is the master-slave dialectic, in which each creates the other.

Intersubjective systems theory: A psychoanalytic phenomenology that claims that all experience originates, is maintained, and may be transformed within the field or system formed by two or more personal subjective worlds of experience.

Intricacy: In Merleau-Ponty, the complexity of embodied intersubjectivity.

Intuition: Immediate knowing without concepts.

Isolated-mind: In Stolorow and Atwood, the modern or Cartesian view that claims foundational reality for the single individual. See, by contrast, *intersubjective systems theory*.

Language game: In Wittgenstein, an informal system of communication, structured by its own rules, within which words have meaning. The same words may mean something else in another language game.

Logical positivism: The view that only statements that can be experimentally verified or falsified have meaning or "cognitive significance."

Materialism: The view that all reality is material.

Meaning-as-use: In Wittgenstein, the view that words gain their meaning from the language-games, or discourses, in which we use them. In another context, the same word may mean something else. There is no essential meaning.

Metaphysics: The philosophical study of reality taken as a whole, or of realities thought to exceed our capacity to know them through the methods of science.

Ontology: The study of being, or of whatever types of being (matter, spirit, and so on) reality is thought to include. In Heidegger, the ontological study of being itself is distinguished from the ontic study of beings that can be enumerated.

Organizing principles: In intersubjective systems theory, basic convictions about who we are and how others are likely to treat us, based on our relational experience. Sometimes called emotional convictions, these principles shape our automatic reactions in widely varied life contexts.

Perceptual faith: In Merleau-Ponty, the sense that the world we perceive, and in which we are intertwined, is more or less as we perceive it.

Phenomenology: The philosophical movement initiated by Edmund Husserl and including, for example, Heidegger, Sartre, Merleau-Ponty, Ricoeur, Gadamer, and Levinas. Despite their many differences, phenomenologists generally attempt to put aside (or "bracket") preconceived ideas and focus as much as possible on experience itself, redescribing a pretheoretical world. Their slogan: "To the things themselves!"

Phronesis: Aristotle's word for practical wisdom (appropriate in politics and ethics), as distinguished from *episteme* (theoretical knowing) and *techne* (knowing how to do or make).

Postmodernism: A cluster of views, mainly French (Derrida, Foucault, Deleuze, Lyotard, and others), that claim to undermine, deconstruct, or unmask modern pretensions to knowing.

Pragmatism: The most important American philosophical movement, including especially Charles Sanders Peirce, William James, and John Dewey. Pragmatists, who tend also to be fallibilists, hold that the meaning of any concept consists in the sum of its conceivable practical effects.

Proprioception: Perception of one's own bodily states and movement in the surrounding space.

Proximity: In Levinas, the ethical claim of the neighbor on me, the other who is both nearest to me and infinitely above me.

Rationalism: The view, often opposed to empiricism, that emphasizes the mind's innate capacity to reach truth.

Reductionism: Any view that replaces complexity with something simpler and thinks that nothing has been lost. An "it all comes down to" approach.

Reification: Treating an abstraction as a thing, or substantive.

Relational psychoanalysis: An American school of thought, indebted both to the interpersonalism of Harry Stack Sullivan and to the British independent group (Fairbairn, Guntrip, and Winnicott). Founded by Stephen Mitchell (1946–2000), this group emphasizes the mutual participation of analyst and patient within a "relational matrix."

Representationalism: The view that mind pictures or describes things in the world. Consciousness is awareness of the resulting mental contents.

Sedimentation: In Merleau-Ponty, the settling of past experience into future expectancies.

Seeing-as: In Wittgenstein, perceiving something *as* something. Rejects the existence of bare sensations.

Selfobject: In Kohutian self psychology, the process of self-consolidation through the relation to an idealized, mirroring, or twin-like other.

Shoah: Hebrew word, meaning "calamity," for what is often called the Holocaust (Greek word for "completely burnt").

Skepticism: Both the basic philosophical attitude of questioning everything and a school of Hellenistic philosophers who made such questioning the center of their thought.

Skilled coping: An expression derived by Hubert Dreyfus from Merleau-Ponty's descriptions of habit and embodiment. Contrasts with both rationalistic and empiricist accounts of knowing.

Solipsism: The self-enclosure that results from isolated-mind thinking. It provides no opportunity to test perceptions or ideas in a community.

Speciesism: Among animal rights advocates, an exaggerated emphasis on the status and prerogatives of the human species.

Substance: A basic entity, in contrast to its attributes. Descartes thought humans were composed of two substances, mind and body.

Substitution: In Levinas, my ethical responsibility to take on the suffering of the other, even to die for the neighbor.

Thrownness: In Heidegger, finding ourselves cast into a world we did not choose.

Vergegnung: In Buber, "mismeeting." An encounter-gone-awry.

Weltlichkeit: In Heidegger, our situated being-in-the-world.

REFERENCES

Adorno, T. (1973). *The jargon of authenticity* (K. Tarnowski & F. Will, Trans.). London: Routledge and Kegan Paul. (Original work published 1964)

Anderson, P. (1972). More is different. *Science, 177*, 393–396.

Aron, L. (1996). *A meeting of minds Mutuality in psychoanalysis*. Hillsdale, NJ: Analytic Press.

Askay, R., & Farquhar, J. (2005). *Apprehending the inaccessible: Freudian psychoanalysis and existential phenomenology*. Evanston, IL: Northwestern University Press.

Atterton, P., Calarco, M., & Friedman, M. S. (2004). *Levinas & Buber: Dialogue & difference*. Pittsburgh, PA: Duquesne University Press.

Atwood, G. E., & Stolorow, R. D. (1984). *Structures of subjectivity: Explorations in psychoanalytic phenomenology*. Hillsdale, NJ: Analytic Press.

Atwood, G. & Stolorow, R. (1993). *Faces in a cloud: Intersubjectivity in personality theory*. Northvale, NJ: Jason Aronson.

Bachant, J. L., & Richards, A. D. (1993). Relational concepts in psychoanalysis: An integration by Stephen A. Mitchell. *Psychoanalytic Dialogues, 3*(3), 431–460.

Bambach, C. (2003). *Heidegger's roots: Nietzsche, national socialism, and the Greeks*. Ithaca: Cornell University Press.

Beebe, B., & Lachmann, F. M. (2001). *Infant research and adult treatment A dyadic systems approach*. Hillsdale, NJ: Analytic Press.

Benjamin, J. (1995). *Like subjects, love objects: Essays on recognition and sexual difference*. New Haven, CT: Yale University Press.

Bergson, H. (1910). *Time and free will: An essay on the immediate data of consciousness* (F. Pogson, Trans.). London: Sonnenschein. (Original work published 1889)

Bernanos, G. (2002). *The diary of a country priest* (P. Morris, Trans.). New York: MacMillian. (Original work published 1936)

Bernasconi, R., & Wood, D. (1988). *The provocation of Levinas: Rethinking the Other*. London: Routledge.

Bernstein, R. J. (2002). *Radical evil: a philosophical interrogation*. Cambridge, UK: Polity Press.

Binswanger, L. (1942). *Grundformen und Erkenntnis menschlichen Daseins*. Zürich, Switzerland: Niehans.

Bouveresse, J. (1995). *Wittgenstein reads Freud: The myth of the unconscious* (C. Cosman, Trans.). Princeton, NJ: Princeton University Press. (Original work published 1991)

Bowlby, J. (1979). *The making & breaking of affectional bonds*. London: Tavistock.

Brandchaft, B., & Stolorow, R. D. (1990). The borderline concept. *Journal of the American Psychoanalytic Association, 38*(4), 1117–1122.

Brothers, D. (2008). *Toward a psychology of uncertainty: Trauma-centered psychoanalysis*. New York: Analytic Press.

Buber, M. (1948). *Das Problem des Menschen*. Heidelberg, Germany: Schneider.

Buber, M. (1957). *Pointing the way*. London: Routledge & Paul. Buber, M. (1962). *Arbres*. Jérusalem: Éditions Ahva.

Buber, M. (1965). *Das dialogische Prinzip*. Heidelberg, Germany: Schneider.

Buber, M. (1967). *A believing humanism: My testament, 1902-1965*. New York: Simon & Schuster.

Buber, M. (1970). *I and Thou* (W. A. Kaufmann, Trans.). New York: Scribner. (Original work published 1923)

Buber, M. (1988). *The knowledge of man: Selected essays*. Atlantic Highlands, NJ: Humanities Press International.

Buber, M. (1991a). *The letters of Martin Buber: A life of dialogue* (N. N. Glatzer & P. R. Mendes-Flohr, Eds.; R. Winston, C. Winston, & H. Zohn, Trans.). New York: Schocken Books.

Buber, M. (1991b). *Tales of the Hasidim*. New York: Schocken Books. (Original work published 1947)

Buber, M. (1999). *Martin Buber on psychology and psychotherapy: Essays, letters, and dialogue* (J. Buber Agassi, Ed.). New York: Syracuse University Press.

Buber, M. (2002). *Between man and man* (R. G. Smith, Trans.). London: Routledge. (Original work published 1947)

Buirski, P., & Haglund, P. (2001). *Making sense together: The intersubjective approach to psychotherapy*. Northvale, NJ: Jason Aronson.

Burston, D., & Frie, R. (2006). *Psychotherapy as a human science*. Pittsburgh, PA: Duquesne University Press.

Camus, A. (1946). *The stranger* (S. Gilbert, Trans.). New York: Knopf. (Original work published 1942)

Carman, T. (2008). *Merleau-Ponty*. Milton Park, England: Routledge.

Carman, T., & Hansen, M. B. N. (2005). *The Cambridge companion to Merleau-Ponty*. Cambridge, England: Cambridge University Press.

Cavell, S. (1990). *Conditions handsome and unhandsome: The constitution of Emersonian perfectionism*. La Salle, IL: Open Court.

Caygill, H. (2002). *Levinas and the political*. London: Routledge.

Chalmers, D. J. (2002). *Philosophy of mind: Classical and contemporary readings*. New York: Oxford University Press.

Chanter, T. (1997). Traumatic response: Levinas's legacy. *Philosophy Today, 41*(Suppl.), 19–27.

Clark, A. (2001). *Mindware: An introduction to the philosophy of cognitive science*. New York: Oxford University Press.

Cohen, R. A. (1986). *Face to face with Levinas*. Albany: State University of New York Press.

Critchley, S. (1991). "Bois"—Derrida's final world on Levinas. In R. Bernasconi & S. Critchley (Eds.), *Re-Reading Levinas* (pp. 162-189). Bloomington: Indiana University Press.

Critchley, S. (1999). *Ethics-politics-subjectivity: Essays on Derrida, Levinas and contemporary French thought*. London: Verso.

Critchley, S. (2002). Introduction. In S. Critchley & R. Bernasconi (Eds.), *The Cambridge Companion to Levinas* (pp. 1-32). Cambridge: Cambridge University Press.

Critchley, S. (2007). *Infinitely demanding: Ethics of commitment, politics of resistance*. London: Verso.

Critchley, S., & Bernasconi, R. (2002). *The Cambridge companion to Levinas*. Cambridge: Cambridge University Press.

Damasio, A. R. (1994). *Descartes' error: Emotion, reason, and the human brain*. New York: Putnam.

Damasio, A. R. (1999). *The feeling of what happens: Body and emotion in the making of consciousness*. New York: Harcourt Brace.

Damasio, A. R. (2003). *Looking for Spinoza: Joy, sorrow, and the feeling brain*. Orlando, FL: Harcourt.

Davey, N. (2006). *Unquiet understanding: Gadamer's philosophical hermeneutics*. Albany: State University of New York Press.

Davis, C. (1996). *Levinas: an introduction*. Notre Dame, Ind.: University of Notre Dame Press.

Derrida, J. (1978). *Writing and difference* (A. Bass, Trans.). Chicago: University of Chicago Press. (Original work published 1967)

Descartes, R., (1996). *Meditations on first philosophy: With selections from the Objections and Replies* (Rev. ed.) (J. Cottingham, & B. Williams, Trans.) New York: Cambridge University Press. (Original work published 1641)

Dillon, M. C. (1997). *Merleau-Ponty's ontology* (2nd ed.). Evanston, IL: Northwestern University Press.

Dilthey, W. (1914). *Gesammelte Schriften*. Leipzig, Germany: Teubner.

Dilthey, W. (1988). *Introduction to the human sciences: An attempt to lay a foundation for the study of society and history* (R. J. Betanzos, Trans.). Detroit, MI: Wayne State University Press. (Original work published 1883)

Dreyfus, H. (2005). Merleau-Ponty and recent cognitive science. In T. Carman & M. Hansen (Eds.), *The Cambridge companion to Merleau-Ponty* (pp. 129–150.). Cambridge, England: Cambridge University Press.

Dreyfus, H. L. (2008). *On the internet* (2nd ed.). London: Routledge.

Duportail, G.-F. (2005). *Intentionnalité et trauma: Lévinas et Lacan*. Paris: L'Harmattan.

Edmonds, D., & Eidinow, J. (2001). *Wittgenstein's poker: The story of a ten-minute argument between two great philosophers*. London: Faber & Faber.

Ehrenberg, D. B. (1992). *The intimate edge: Extending the reach of psychoanalytic interaction*. New York: Norton.

Eisold, B. K. (1999). Profound recognition. *Contemporary Psychoanalysis, 35*(1), 107–130.

Etchegoyen, R. H. (1991). *The fundamentals of psychoanalytic technique.* London: Karnac Books.

Fonagy, P., Gergely, G., Jurist, E. L., & Target, M. (2002). *Affect regulation, mentalization, and the development of the self.* New York: Other Press.

Frank, M. (1992). *Stil in der Philosophie.* Stuttgart, Germany: Reclam.

Frie, R. (2002). Modernism or postmodernism? *Contemporary Psychoanalysis, 38*(4), 635–673.

Frie, R. (2003). *Understanding experience: Psychotherapy and postmodernism.* London: Routledge.

Frie, R., & Orange, D. M. (2009). *Beyond postmodernism: New dimensions in theory and practice.* London: Routledge.

Frie, R., & Reis, B. (2001). Understanding intersubjectivity: Psychoanalytic formulations and their philosophical underpinnings. *Contemporary Psychoanalysis, 37,* 297–327.

Friedman, M. S. (1994). *The healing dialogue in psychotherapy.* Northvale, NJ: Jason Aronson.

Friedman, M. S. (2002). *Martin Buber: The life of dialogue* (4th ed.). London: Routledge.

Fuller, R. W. (2006). *All rise: Somebodies, nobodies, and the politics of dignity.* San Francisco: Berrett-Koehler.

Gadamer, H.-G. (1976). *Philosophical hermeneutics* (D. Linge, Trans.) Berkeley: University of California Press.

Gadamer, H.-G. (1980). *Dialogue and dialectic: Eight hermeneutical studies on Plato* (P. Smith, Trans.) New Haven, CT: Yale University Press.

Gadamer, H.-G. (1982). *Reason in the age of science* (F. Lawrence, Trans.) Cambridge, MA: MIT Press.

Gadamer, H.-G. (1985). *Gesammelte Werke.* 10 Baende.Tübingen: Mohr.

Gadamer, H.-G. (1985). *Philosophical apprenticeships* (R. Sullivan, Trans.) Cambridge, MA: MIT Press.

Gadamer, H.-G. (1989). *Truth and method* (2nd ed.). New York: Crossroad.

Gadamer, H.-G. (1991). *Truth and method* (J. Weinsheimer & D. Marshall, Trans. 2nd ed.). New York: Crossroads. (Original work published 1960)

Gadamer, H.-G., Dutt, C., & Palmer, R. E. (2001). *Gadamer in conversation: Reflections and commentary.* New Haven, CT: Yale University Press.

Gadamer, H.-G. (2003). *A century of philosophy.* (R. Dottori, Ed.) New York: Continuum.

Gadamer, H.-G. (2007). *The Gadamer reader: A bouquet of the later writings* (R. Palmer, Ed.) Evanston, Ill.: Northwestern University Press.

Gadamer, H.-G., & Hahn, L. E. (1997). *The philosophy of Hans-Georg Gadamer.* Chicago: Open Court.

Gallagher, S. (2005). *How the body shapes the mind.* Oxford, England: Clarendon Press.

Gallagher, S., & Zahavi, D. (2008). *The phenomenological mind: An introduction to philosophy of mind and cognitive science.* London: Routledge.

Gendlin, E. (1979). *Befindlichkeit*: Heidegger and the philosophy of psychology. *Review of Existential Psychology & Psychiatry, 16*, 43–71.

Gendlin, E. T. (1996). *Focusing-oriented psychotherapy: A manual of the experiential method.* New York: Guilford Press.

Genova, J. (1995). *Wittgenstein: A way of seeing.* New York: Routledge.

Gladwell, M. (2008). *Outliers: The story of success.* New York: Little, Brown.

Grondin, J.(2003). *Hans-Georg Gadamer: A biography* (J. Weinsheimer, Trans.) New Haven, CT: Yale University Press.(Original work published 1999)

Habermas, J. (1984). *The theory of communicative action* (T. McCourt, Trans.) Boston: Beacon Press. (Original work published 1981)

Habermas, J. (1990). *Moral consciousness and communicative action* (C. Lenhardt & S Nicholsen, Trans.) Cambridge, MA: MIT Press. (Original work published 1983)

Hacking, I. (1999). *The social construction of what?* Cambridge, Mass: Harvard University Press.

Hale, N. G. (1995). *The rise and crisis of psychoanalysis in the United States: Freud and the Americans, 1917-1985.* New York: Oxford University Press.

Heidegger, M. (1962). *Being and time* (J. Macquarrie & E. Robinson, Trans.) New York: Harper. (Original work published 1927)

Heidegger, M. (1977). *Basic writings: From* Being and Time *(1927) to* The Task of Thinking *(1964).* (D. Krell, Ed.) New York: Harper & Row.

Heidegger, M.(1998). *Pathmarks.* (W. McNeill, Ed.) Cambridge, England: Cambridge University Press.

Heidegger, M. (2001). *Zollikon seminars: protocols, conversations, letters* (F. Mayr & R. Askay, Trans.). Evanston, Ill.: Northwestern University Press. (Original work published 1987)

Heidegger, M., & McNeill, W. (1998). *Pathmarks.* Cambridge, England: Cambridge University Press.

Herzog, P. (1988). The myth of Freud as anti-philosopher. In P. E. Stepansky (Ed.), *Freud: appraisals and reappraisals* (pp. 163–189). Hillsdale, NJ: Analytic Press.

Hoffman, I. Z. (2001). Reply to reviews by Slavin, Stein, and Stern. *Psychoanalytic Dialogues, 11*(3), 469–497.

Husserl, E. (1964). *The phenomenology of internal time-consciousness.* (J. Church, Trans.) Bloomington: Indiana University Press. (Original work published 1928)

Husserl, E. (1982). *Ideas pertaining to a pure phenomenology and to a phenomenological philosophy* (W. Boyce Gibson, Trans.) The Hague: Nijhoff. (Original work published 1913)

Hutchison, J. A. (1977). *Living options in world philosophy.* Honolulu: University Press of Hawaii.

Hycner, R., & Jacobs, L. (1995). *The healing relationship in Gestalt therapy: A dialogic/self-psychological approach.* Highland, NY: Gestalt Journal Press.

Irigaray, L., & Whitford, M. (1991). *The Irigaray reader.* Cambridge, MA: Basil Blackwell.

Jaenicke, C. (2008). *The risk of relatedness: Intersubjectivity theory in clinical practice*. Lanham, MD: Jason Aronson.

Janik, A., & Toulmin, S. E. (1973). *Wittgenstein's Vienna*. New York: Simon & Schuster.

Kafka, F. (1996). *The metamorphosis: Translation, backgrounds and contexts, criticism*. (S. Corngold, Ed.) New York: Norton. (Original work published 1915)

Karen, R. (1994). *Becoming attached: Unfolding the mystery of the infant-mother bond and its impact on later life*. New York: Warner Books.

Kohut, H. (1959). Introspection, empathy, and psychoanalysis. *Journal of the American Psychoanalytic Association, 7*, 459–483.

Kohut, H.(1984). *How does analysis cure?* (A. Goldberg & P. Stepansky, Eds.) Chicago: University of Chicago Press.

Kohut, H.(1996). *Heinz Kohut: The Chicago Institute lectures*. (P. Tolpin & M. Tolpin, Eds.) Hillsdale, NJ: Analytic Press.

Lawn, C. (2006). *Gadamer: A guide for the perplexed*. London: Continuum.

Lear, J. (2006). *Radical hope: Ethics in the face of cultural devastation*. Cambridge, MA: Harvard University Press.

LeDoux, J. E. (1996). *The emotional brain: The mysterious underpinnings of emotional life*. New York: Simon & Schuster.

Levenson, E. A. (1996). Aspects of self-revelation and self-disclosure. *Contemporary Psychoanalysis, 32,* 237.

Levin, D. (1998). Tracework: Myself and others in the moral phenomenology of Merleau-Ponty and Levinas. *International Journal of Philosophical Studies, 6,* 345–392.

Levinas, E. (1934/1990). Reflections on the philosophy of Hitlerism. *Critical Inquiry, 17,* 62–71.

Levinas, E. (1969). *Totality and infinity: An essay on exteriority* (A. Lingis, Trans.) Pittsburgh, PA: Duquesne University Press.(Original work published 1961)

Levinas, E. (1973). *The theory of intuition in Husserl's phenomenology*. Evanston, IL: Northwestern University Press.

Levinas, E. (1981). *Otherwise than being: Or, beyond essence* (A. Lingis, Trans.) Boston: Nijhoff.(Original work published 1974)

Levinas, E. (1987). *Collected philosophical papers* (A. Lingis, Trans.) Boston: Nijhoff.

Levinas, E. (1989). *The Levinas reader* (S. Hand, Ed.). Oxford, England: Blackwell.

Levinas, E. (1990). *Difficult freedom: Essays on Judaism* (S. Hand, Trans.) Baltimore: Johns Hopkins University Press. (Original work published 1963)

Levinas, E. (1994). *Outside the subject* (M. Smith, Trans.) Stanford, CA: Stanford University Press. (Original work published 1987)

Levinas, E. (1996). *Emmanuel Levinas: Basic philosophical writings* (Peperzak, A. T., Critchley, S., & Bernasconi, R. Bloomington, Eds.). Indiana University Press.

Levinas, E. (1998a). *Collected philosophical papers*. Pittsburgh, PA: Duquesne University Press.

Levinas, E. (1998b). *Entre nous: On thinking-of-the-other*. New York: Columbia University Press.

Levinas, E. (1998c). *Otherwise than being, or, Beyond essence*. Pittsburgh, PA: Duquesne University Press.

Levinas, E. (2000). *God, death, and time* (B. Bergo, Trans.) Stanford, CA: Stanford University Press. (Original work published 1993)

Levinas, E., (2001). *Is it righteous to be? Interviews with Emmanuel Lévinas* (J. Robbins, Ed.). Stanford, CA: Stanford University Press.

Levinas, E., & Nemo, P. (1985). *Ethics and infinity*. Pittsburgh, PA: Duquesne University Press.

Levinas, E., & Smith, M. B. (1993). *Outside the subject*. London: Athlone.

Malka, S. (2006). *Emmanuel Levinas: His life and legacy*. Pittsburgh, PA: Duquesne University Press.

McGinn, M. (1997). *Routledge philosophy guidebook to Wittgenstein and the philosophical investigations*. London: Routledge.

Melchert, N. (2002). *The great conversation: A historical introduction to philosophy* (4th ed.). Boston: McGraw-Hill.

Merleau-Ponty, M. (1963). *The structure of behavior* (A. Fisher, Trans.) Boston: Beacon Press. (Original work published 1942)

Merleau-Ponty, M. (1964a). *The primacy of perception, and other essays on phenomenological psychology, the philosophy of art, history, and politics*. (J. Edie, Ed.) Evanston, IL: Northwestern University Press.

Merleau-Ponty, M. (1964b). *Sense and non-sense* (H. Dreyfus, Trans.) Evanston, IL: Northwestern University Press.

Merleau-Ponty, M. (1964c). *Signs* (R. McCleary, Trans.) Evanston, IL: Northwestern University Press. (Original work published 1960)

Merleau-Ponty, M. (1968). *The visible and the invisible, followed by working notes*. (C. LeFort, Ed.) Evanston, IL: Northwestern University Press. (Original work published 1964)

Merleau-Ponty, M. (1969). *The essential writings of Merleau-Ponty* (A. Fisher, Ed.) New York: Harcourt.

Merleau-Ponty, M. (1973). *Adventures of the dialectic* (J. Bien, Trans.) Evanston, IL: Northwestern University Press. (Original work published 1955).

Merleau-Ponty, M. (1980). *Humanism and terror: An essay on the Communist problem* (J. O'Neill, Trans.) Westport, CT: Greenwood Press.(Original work published 1947)

Merleau-Ponty, M. (2002). *Phenomenology of perception* (C. Smith, Trans.). London: Routledge. (Original work published 1945)

Merleau-Ponty, M. (2004). *The world of perception* (O. Davis, Trans.) London: Routledge. (Original work published 1948)

Mill, J. S. (1880). *Ueber Frauenemancipation; Plato; Arbeiterfrage; Socialismus* (S. Freud, Trans.) Leipzig, Germany: Fues's Verlag (R. Reisland).

Mitchell, S. A. (1988). *Relational concepts in psychoanalysis: An integration*. Cambridge, MA: Harvard University Press.

Mitchell, S. A. (1993). *Hope and dread in psychoanalysis.* New York: Basic Books.

Monk, R. (1990). *Ludwig Wittgenstein: The duty of genius.* New York: Free Press.

Moran, D. (2000). *Introduction to phenomenology.* London: Routledge.

Nagel, T. (1974). What is it like to be a bat? *Philosophical Review, 83,* 435-450.

Neiman, S. (2002). *Evil in modern thought: An alternative history of philosophy.* Princeton, N.J.: Princeton University Press.

Nietzsche, F. (1966). *Beyond Good and Evil* (W. Kaufmann, Trans.). New York: Random House. (Original work published 1886)

Ogden, T. H. (1997). *Reverie and interpretation: Sensing something human.* Northvale, NJ: Jason Aronson.

Orange, D. M. (1984). *Peirce's conception of God: A developmental study.* Lubbock, TX: Institute for Studies in Pragmaticism.

Orange, D. M. (1995). *Emotional understanding: Studies in psychoanalytic epistemology.* New York: Guilford Press.

Orange, D. (2002). There is no outside: Empathy and authenticity in psychoanalytic process. *Psychoanalytic Psychology, 19,* 686–700.

Orange, D. (2003, November). *Trauma, dissociation, and the loss of complexity.* Paper presented at the International Association for Psychoanalytic Self Psychology, 26th annual Conference on the Psychology of the Self. Chicago.

Orange, D. (2006). For whom the bell tolls: Context, complexity, and compassion in psychoanalysis. *International Journal of Psychoanalytic Self Psychology, 1,* 5–21.

Orange, D. (2008a). Radical hope: Ethics in the face of cultural devastation. *Psychoanalytic Psychology, 25,* 368–374.

Orange, D. (2008b). Recognition as: Intersubjective vulnerability in the psychoanalytic dialogue *International Journal of Psychoanalytic Self Psychology, 3,* 178–194.

Orange, D. (2008c). Whose shame is it anyway? Lifeworlds of humiliation and systems of restoration. *Contemporary Psychoanalysis, 44,* 83–100.

Orange, D. (2009a). Kohut Memorial Lecture: Attitudes, values, and intersubjective vulnerability. *International Journal of Psychoanalytic Self Psychology, 4,* 235-253.

Orange, D. (2009b). Psychoanalysis in a phenomenological spirit. *International Journal of Psychoanalytic Self Psychology, 4,* 119-121.

Orange, D. (2009c). Toward the art of the living dialogue: Between constructivism and hermeneutics in psychoanalytic thinking. In R. Frie & D. Orange (Eds.), *Beyond Postmodernism: New Dimensions in Clinical Theory and Practice* (pp. 117-142). London: Routledge.

Orange, D. (in press). Speaking the unspeakable: Traumatic living memory and the dialogue of metaphors. *International Journal of Psychoanalytic Self Psychology.*

Orange, D. M., Atwood, G. E., & Stolorow, R. D. (1997). *Working intersubjectively: Contextualism in psychoanalytic practice.* Hillsdale, NJ: Analytic Press.

Palmer, R. (2002). A response to Richard Wolin on Gadamer and the Nazis. *International Journal of Philosophical Studies, 10,* 467-482.

Pascal, B. (2008). *Pensées and other writings.* (H. Levi, Ed.) Oxford, England: Oxford University Press.

PBS (Producer). (2008). *Inheritance.* Podcast retrieved from http://www.pbs.org/pov/pov2008/inheritance/.

Peirce, C. S. (1960). *Collected papers.* Cambridge, MA: Harvard University Press.

Perls, F. S. (1969). *Gestalt therapy verbatim.* Lafayette, Calif.: Real People Press.

Plato. (1997). *Complete works* (J. M. Cooper & D. S. Hutchinson, Eds.). Indianapolis, IN: Hackett.

Preston, L., & Shumsky, E. (2002). From an empathic stance to an empathic dance. *Progress in Self Psychology, 18,* 47-61.

Rawls, J. (1971). *A theory of justice.* Cambridge, MA: Harvard University Press.

Regan, T., & Singer, P. (1989). *Animal rights and human obligations* (2nd ed.). Englewood Cliffs, NJ: Prentice Hall.

Rhees, R. (1984). *Recollections of Wittgenstein: Hermine Wittgenstein, Fania Pascal, F.R. Leavis, John King, M. O'C. Drury.* Oxford, England: Oxford University Press.

Ricoeur, P. (1965). *History and truth* (C. Kelbley, Trans.) Evanston, IL: Northwestern University Press. (Original work published 1955)

Ricoeur, P. (1970). *Freud and philosophy: An essay on interpretation* (D. Savage, Trans.) New Haven, CT: Yale University Press. (Original work published 1965)

Ricoeur, P. (1992). *Oneself as another* (K. Blamey, Trans.) Chicago: University of Chicago Press. (Original work published 1990)

Risser, J. (1997). *Hermeneutics and the voice of the other.* Albany: State University of New York Press.

Rogers, C. R. (1961). *On becoming a person: A therapist's view of psychotherapy.* Boston: Houghton Mifflin.

Rosenzweig, F. (2005). *The star of redemption* (B. Galli, Ed.) Madison: University of Wisconsin Press. (Original work published 1919)

Rowling, J. K. (1999). *Harry Potter and the chamber of secrets.* New York: Levine Books.

Russell, B. (1968). *The autobiography of Bertrand Russell.* Toronto, Ontario, Canada: McClelland & Stewart.

Ryle, G. (1959). *The concept of mind.* New York: Barnes & Noble.

Sartre, J.-P. (1975). *Situations* (B. Eisler, Trans.) Paris: Gallimard. (Original work published 1964)

Sartre, J.-P. (1977). *Life/situations: Essays written and spoken.* New York: Pantheon Books.

Sartre, J.-P.(1979). *Nausea* (L. Alexander, Trans.) Cambridge, MA: Bentley. Original work published 1938)

Sartre, J.-P., & Alexander, L. (1979). *Nausea.* Cambridge, MA: Bentley.

Sass, L. A. (1989). Humanism, hermeneutics, and humanistic psychoanalysis: Differing conceptions of subjectivity. *Psychoanalysis and Contemporary Thought, 12,* 433-504.

Schilpp, P. A., Friedman, M. S., & Buber, M. (1967). *The philosophy of Martin Buber*. La Salle, IL: Open Court.

Schleiermacher, F. (1998). *Hermeneutics and criticism and other writings* (A. Bowie, Ed. & Trans.). Cambridge, England: Cambridge University Press.

Schleiermacher, F., & Frank, M. (1977). *Hermeneutik und Kritik: mit e. Anh. sprachphilos. Texte Schleiermachers*. Frankfurt am Main: Suhrkamp.

Scholem, G. G. (1995). *Major trends in Jewish mysticism*. New York: Schocken Books.

Schopenhauer, A. (1969). *The world as will and representation* (E. Payne, Trans.) New York: Dover. (Original work published 1819)

Shotter, J. (2008). Wittgenstein and the everyday: From radical hiddenness to "nothing is hidden": From representation to participation [Draft for *Journal of Mundane Behavior*]. Retrieved from http://pubpages.unh.edu/~jds/JMB.htm

Siegel, D. J. (1999). *The developing mind: How relationships and the brain interact to shape who we are*. New York: Guilford Press.

Singer, P. (1986). *In defense of animals*. New York: Perennial Library.

Sluga, H. (1996a). Ludwig Wittgenstein: Life and work. In H. Sluga & D. Stern (Eds.), *The Cambridge Companion to Wittgenstein* (pp. 1-33). Cambridge: Cambridge University Press.

Sluga, H. (1996a). "Whose house is that?" Wittgenstein on the self. In H. Sluga & D. Stern (Eds.), *The Cambridge Companion to Wittgenstein* (pp. 320-353). Cambridge: Cambridge University Press.

Staemmler, F.-M. (2007). The willingness to be uncertain: Preliminary thoughts about interpretation and understanding in gestalt therapy. *International Gestalt journal, 29*, 11–42.

Staemmler, F.-M. (2009). *Das Geheimnis des Anderen--Empathie in der Psychotherapie—Wie Therapeuten und Klienten einander verstehen*. Stuttgart: Klett-Cotta.

Steele, R. S. (1979). Psychoanalysis and hermeneutics. *International Journal of Psycho-Analysis, 6*, 389–411.

Stern, D. B. (1997). *Unformulated experience: From dissociation to imagination in psychoanalysis*. Hillsdale, NJ: Analytic Press.

Stern, D. N. (2004). *The present moment in psychotherapy and everyday life*. New York: Norton.

Stolorow, R. D. (2000). From isolated minds to experiential worlds: An intersubjective space odyssey. *American Journal of Psychotherapy, 54*(2), 149–151.

Stolorow, R. D. (2007). *Trauma and human existence: Autobiographical, psychoanalytic, and philosophical reflections*. New York: Analytic Press.

Stolorow, R., & Atwood, G. E. (1992). *Contexts of being: The intersubjective foundations of psychological life*. Hillsdale, NJ: Analytic Press.

Stolorow, R., Atwood, G. E., & Brandchaft, B. (1987). *Psychoanalytic treatment: An intersubjective approach*. Hillsdale, NJ: The Analytic Press.

Stolorow, R., Atwood, G. E., & Orange, D. (in press). Heidegger's Nazism and the hypostatization of being. *International Journal of Psychoanalytic Self Psychology*.

Stolorow, R., Orange, D. M., & Atwood, G. E. (1998). Projective identification begone! Commentary on paper by Susan H. Sands. *Psychoanalytic Dialogues, 8*(5), 719–725.

Taylor, C. (1985). *Philosophy and the human sciences*. Cambridge, England: Cambridge University Press.

Tolstoy, L., & Hapgood, I. F. (2008). *The Gospel in brief*. Mineola, NY: Dover.

Trüb, H. (1952). *Heilung aus der Begegnung: Eine Auseinandersetzung mit der Psychologie C.G. Jungs*. Stuttgart, Germany: Ernst Klett Verlag.

Twain, M. (2003). *A tramp abroad*. New York: Modern Library. (Original work published 1880)

Vogel, L. (1994). *The fragile "we": Ethical implications of Heidegger's Being and Time*. Evanston, IL: Northwestern University Press.

Warnke, G. (1987). *Gadamer: Hermeneutics, tradition, and reason*. Stanford, Calif.: Stanford University Press.

Warnke, G. (2002). Hermeneutics, ethics, and politics. In R. Dostal (Ed.), *The Cambridge Companion to Gadamer* (pp. 79-101). Cambridge, UK: Cambridge University Press.

Weininger, O. (1906). *Sex & character*. London: Heinemann. (Original work published 1903)

Winnicott, D. W. (1971). *Playing and reality*. New York: Basic Books.

Wittgenstein, L. (1953). *Philosophical investigations*. New York: Macmillan.

Wittgenstein, L. (1969). *Preliminary studies for the "Philosophical investigations," generally known as the blue and brown books* (2nd ed.). Oxford, England: Blackwell.

Wittgenstein, L. (1980). *Remarks on the philosophy of psychology*. (G. Anscombe, G. Wright, & H. Nyman, Eds.) Chicago: University of Chicago Press.

Wittgenstein, L. (2001). *Tractatus logico-philosophicus*. (D. Pears & B. McGuiness, Eds.) Atlantic Highlands, NJ: Humanities Press.

Wittgenstein, L., Anscombe, G. E. M., & von Wright, G. H. (1969). *On certainty*. Oxford, England: Blackwell.

Wittgenstein, L., Wright, G. H. v., & Anscombe, G. E. M. (1979). *Notebooks, 1914-1916* (2nd ed.). Chicago: University of Chicago Press.

Wolin, R. (2002). The complicities of Hans-Georg Gadamer: Untruth and method. *New Republic, 4*, 36-45.

Yontef, G. (1988). *Awareness, dialogue and process: Essays on gestalt therapy*. Gouldsboro, ME: Gestalt Journal Press.

Zahavi, D. (2005). *Subjectivity and selfhood: Investigating the first-person perspective*. Cambridge, MA: MIT Press.

INDEX

A

Acknowledgement, 28
Actual (nonneurotic) guilt, 29
Advent, 67
Affectivity or *Befindlichkeit*, 62, 78
Aggression, 3, 51, 82, 95, 111, 116
Allport, Gordon, 8
Alterity, 85, 121
Ambiguity, 70, 71, 121
Ambiguous, 24, 67, 70, 121
Anerkennung, 28
Aristotle, 43, 108, 117
Aron, Lewis, 81
Asian religion, 24
Aspect-blindness, 51
Asymmetrical ethical relation, 94
Attachment systems, 3
Attachment theories, 106, 121
Attitude, 108, 114
Attunement, 64
Atwood, George, 45, 113–114
Authenticity (*Eigentlichkeit,
       Jemeinigkeit*), 66, 88–90, 95
Authoritarian, 10, 51, 95, 105, 106
Automaticity, 4, 5–6, 65
Autrui (other). *See* Other (*Autrui*)

B

Background
    emotional convictions, 113
    hermeneutic dialogue, 109
    nonverbal, 14
    in perception, 73
    receded into, 12
    theory made invisible or relegated
       to, 5

Western philosophy history, 1
Background contexts, 50
Beebe, Beatrice 64
Befindlichkeit, 62, 78, 121
Behavior
    emotions and feelings, 47
    pain-language, 44
    and perception study, 58
    post-traumatic stress disorder, 29
Behaviorist, 6, 43, 46, 56, 58
Being and Time (Heidegger), 12, 59, 78,
       88, 108
Being-in-relation, 32
Being-in-the-world
    and authenticity, 89
    and belonging, 96
    Buber vs Heidegger, 30, 32
    defined, 121
    distinguish ontological from ontic,
       26
    and the face, 82
    and humanism, 7
    Merleau-Ponty vs Heidegger, 11
    reifications of experiential qualities
       of, 72
    and skilled coping, 64
    studied by Levinas, 78
    and studies of perceptual processes,
       59
Believing humanism, 18, 31–33
Bergson, Henri, 78
Bernanos, Georges, 90
Bernasconi, Robert, 92
Bernstein, Richard, 87
Bestätigung (English: confirmation), 28.
       See Confirmation

Bifurcation, 60
Binding expectations, 111
Binswanger, Ludwig, 3, 16, 20, 89
Body-in-the-world, 57
Body-subject
    defined, 121
    embodied intersubjectivity, 10, 58
    and human life, 70
    neglected resource, 11
    and prereflective level in world, 68
    skilled coping, 64
    and subjectivity, 69
Brahms, Johannes, 36
Brentano, Franz, 3, 87–88
Buber, Martin
    antireductionism, 30–31
    challenged Freud and Jung, 15
    confirmation, 27–30
    on Descartes, 23
    de-Socratizing philosophers, 23
    existential-humanist children/
        grandchildren of, 3
    as humanist, 31–33
    and humanistic psychotherapists, 15
    I and Thou, 18–24
    inclusion, 24–27
    I-Thou encounter, 15
    and Levinas, 90–92
    life and work, 16–17
    and Merleau-Ponty, 68
    moral status of animals, 8
    vs Heidegger, 30, 32
    vs Jung, 16
    vs Wittgenstein, 35
    works of:
        Das Problem des Menschen, 16
        I and Thou, 9, 17, 21, 34
        Martin Buber on Psychology and
            Psychotherapy, 34
        Tales of the Hasidim, 17
Burns, Robert, 70

C

Calarco, Matthew, 31–32
Camus, Albert, 71
Carman, Taylor, 64, 65
Cartesian
    cogito, 10
    container-mind concept, 69
    dogmatic rationalism of, 67

intellectualism, 56
mind, 44
mind-body dualism, 55
subjectivism, 6–7
Categorical imperative, 33, 121
Cause, 43, 47–48, 59, 61, 121
Cavell, Marcia, 13
Cavell, Stanley, 108
Chaos Theory, 5, 28, 58, 71
Chalmers, David, 61
Chanter, Tina, 91
Chiasm, 57, 75, 87, 121
Clark, Andy, 59-60
Clinical work
    compassionate, 114
    constructive resources for, 108–114
    ethical task, 52
    and patient's language, 103
    psychoanalysis, 43
    and skilled coping, 65
    themes of, 62–64
    trauma as experience, 84
    traumatic testimony, 85–86
    vs theories, 3
Clinicians
    care about thinking, 4
    challenges for, 1
    conceptual supports, 50–52
    conceptual tools, 43
    devastation left by psychological
        trauma, 71
    and emotional life, 68–69
    fear of theory and philosophy, 4
    ideals resemble Socrates, 2
    intersubjectivity, 75
    intimacy of therapeutic encounter, 18
    leading edge, 67
    meaning-as-use, 10
    patient, 14
    psychoanalytic tradition, 94–95
    and skilled coping, 64–65
    spiritual discipline reading
        Wittgenstein, 53
    trauma, 83
Cogito, 10, 60, 121
Cognitive behaviorists, 56
Cognitive neuroscience, 60–62
Cognitive science, 121
Coming-to-an-understanding
    (Verständigung), 118

Communication. *See also* Language-
    game (*Sprachspiel*)
    authoritarian, 105
    and language, 22–23
    objectification, 71
    systems of, 40, 68
Communion, 21, 68
Compassion, 114–117
Complexity
    intricacy, 71
    language-game, 51–52
    of meanings, 41
    prevents reduction/judgmental
        attitudes, 116
    reductionism, 14, 42, 50
    split world, 73
    Wittgenstein valued context and, 44
Complexity theory, 5, 31, 58
Conception of cure, 52
Conceptual tools, 43
Concreteness, 24, 25
Confirmation, 15, 16, 27–30, 122
Consciousness, 57, 74, 109
Construction, 113, 122
Constructivism, 122
Contact
    aspect-blindness, 51
    defined, 122
    dialogic, 18
    Gestalt therapy, 40
    with ourselves, 70
    person-to-person, 15
    proximity, 93
    reach for, 94
    real, 20
Container-mind concept, 69, 47-48
Contextualism, 40, 47
Contextualizing, 104
Conversation
    dialogue, 104–105
    implicit critique, 107
    makes us human, 117
    perspectival realism, 25
    philosophical activity, 101
    and reasons, 47–48
    understanding, 11–12, 105
Creativity, 5
Critchley, Simon, 79, 83, 85
Criterion of truth, 70
Critique of objectifying reductions, 82
Cultural expressions, 67

D

Damasio, Antonio, 59, 61
Darwin, Charles, 7, 96
Dasein, 7, 23, 78, 89, 108. *See also* Being-
    in-the-world
Das Problem des Menschen (Buber), 16
das Zwischenmenschliche , 24
Deconstruction, 113, 122
Derrida, Jacques, 79, 84
Descartes
    Buber on, 23
    causes and events, 59
    criterion of truth, 70
    dualisms of, 72
    idea of infinity, 97
    Merleau-Ponty lived in shadow of, 55
    methodical doubt, 58
    private-language argument, 44
    and understanding consciousness, 60
Descriptive phenomenology, 111
De-Socratizing philosophers, 23
Details, 63–64
Determinism, 122
Devastation, 21, 71
Developmental achievement, 19, 75
Diagnostic labeling, 111
Dialectic, 70, 88, 122
Dialogic
    for clinical understanding, 11
    contact, 18
    context of Gadamer's work, 101
    effort to notice aspects of things, 50
    ethics, 32
    form of human connection, 91
    hermeneutics, 108, 110, 116, 117
    inclusion (*umfassung*), 24, 25, 51, 105
    and language, 23
    partner, 10, 28
    path is risky, 21
    philosophy, 12, 109
    process and compassion, 115
    reciprocity and equality, 92
    reflection, 94
    relation and I-You, 30
    therapies, 6
    and thinking, 7
    thinking and writing form of
        Wittgenstein, 38
    understanding, 99, 102, 104, 112
Dialogic encounter, 20, 33

Dialogic hermeneutics, 108, 109
Dialogic inclusion, 25, 51, 105
Dialogic partner, 10, 28
Dialogic philosophy, 109
Dialogic work
  experiential world, 110
  finding meaning within contexts, 10
  and intimate contact, 18
  notice aspects of things, 50
  solicitude, 23
  and surprise, 20, 23
  thinking and writing form of
    Wittgenstein, 38–39
  working in the dark, 21
Dialogue
  authenticity through, 89
  Buber's life of, 91
  and communication, 68
  confirm, 28
  contribution of Buber, 15
  conversation, 104–105
  empathic, 9
  genuine human, 31
  hermeneutics, 109
  in hermeneutic spirit, 14
  humanistic psychotherapies, 16
  humanistic tradition, 8
  I and Thou philosophy, 10
  I-It relations, 92
  internal, 38
  intersubjectivity, 75
  I-You, 27
  meanings to emerge in, 113
  organizing principles, 111
  between phenomenology and
    cognitive neuroscience, 62
  with philosophers, 2
  thinker's questions/insights into, 5
  and true contact, 20
  understanding and, 12
  understanding emergent in, 101, 107
  vs Dasein's solicitude, 23, 66
Dialogue (Gesprächspartner), 28
Dilthey, Wilhelm, 6, 26, 47, 103–104
Dissociation, 14, 64, 116
Dogmatic rationalism, 67
Dogmatism, 12, 122
Dostoyevsky, Fyodor, 85, 86, 95
Double asymmetry, 70
Dreyfus, Hubert, 60
Du, 18, 32, 33, 92

Dualism. See also specific types
  and ambiguous, 70
  attack on, 42
  complexity, 71
  defined, 122
  and experiential absoluteness, 73
  of implicit and explicit, 72
  of in-itself and for-itself, 56
  inside-outside opposition, 60
  language-games, 46–47
  mind and body, 44
  mind-body, 55
  and sedimentation, 65
  study of lived experience, 59
  types of, 44, 58, 72

E

École Normale Israelite Orientale
    (ENIO), 79
Efficient causes, 43
Ehrenberg, Darlene, 15
Eigentlichkeit, Jemeinigkeit
    (authenticity), 66, 89
Einfühlung (empathy), 24, 26, 104, 106
Emanation, 82, 122
Emmanuel, Levinas (Malka), 97
Embodied intersubjectivity, 10, 33, 58,
    61, 73, 75
Embodiment
  defined, 122
  experience, 69
  lived and living experience, 72
  perception, 58
  philosophy of, 59
  social world, 68
  worlded, 61
EMDR (eye-movement desensitization
    and reprocessing), 6
Emotion, 68–69
Emotional availability, 93, 116
Emotional convictions, 65, 113
Emotional life, 68–69
Emotional memory, 72
Emotions and feeling, 47, 60, 64, 72–73
Empathy, 24, 87–88, 104, 105, 106
Empirical sciences and perception, 60
Empiricism, 56, 67, 122
Epiphenomenon, 11
Episteme (theoretical knowing), 117
Epistemology, 122

Equality, 33, 39, 41
Erlebnis (event experience), 102
Essence, 27, 40, 42, 122
Essentialism, 42, 97
Ethical humanism, 95–97
Ethical relation, 92
Ethical task, 36, 52
Ethics
    and aggression, 82
    asymmetry of Levinasian, 87
    defined, 122
    dialogic, 32
    of equality and justice, 33
    exhaustion (burnout), 95
    as first philosophy, 11
    Heidegger's evasion of, 31
    height of other, 80
    ideas express primacy of, 93–95
    is first philosophy, 79
    Kantian-inspired justice, 106
    moral phenomenology, 71
    obligations and authenticity, 89
    perfectionist, 108
    and politics, 117
    relation is asymmetrical, 81, 92
    Rosenzweig taught religious studies
        and, 17
    and self, 86–87
    Stoics established an, 8
    and traumatism, 85
    Wittgenstein's thinking subject and,
        52
Ethics and Infinity (Levinas), 97
Event experience vs accumulated
        learning, 102
Exhaustion (burnout), 95
Existential guilt, 29
Existentialism, 7, 89, 122
Existential phenomenology, 74
Existential psychotherapies, 100
Experience
    aspect-blindness, 51
    attunement, 64
    authenticity, 66
    and child's behavior, 58
    clinical, 4, 5, 90
    container-mind concept, 69
    from different points of view, 49
    embodied, 55, 65, 71
    embodiment and, 72
    emotional, 114

first-person, 48
human, 9
inclusion, 24
intersubjective constitution of, 87
intersubjective systems theory, 75
intrinsically social, 46
irreducibility, 93
I-You, 19, 25, 27, 31
in and of lifeworld, 11
lived, 59, 61, 78
other's, 70
patient's, 6, 22, 111, 115, 116
personal, 6, 14, 82
of psychoanalytic work, 113
and reductionism, 47
reformation of, 95
relational, 112
religious, 15
self, 30
self-enclosed notion of, 44
sense, 67
traumatic, 84, 85, 86
from viewpoint of embodied
        perception, 60
what-is-it-like-ness, 62
Experience-distant, 57
Experience-distant description, 31
Experience is holistic, 59
Experience-near concepts, 94
Experiential world, 65, 72, 110, 111, 112,
    115

F

Face, 97
Face of the other, 33, 47, 80, 83, 92, 118
Fairbairn, W. R. D., 1
Fallibilism, 5–6, 11, 123
Family resemblances, 10, 42, 43, 50, 123
Feminists, 13
Final causes, 43
Flesh, 10, 57, 70, 75
Flesh (*le chair*), 74, 123
Fly-bottle, 50, 51
Frankl, Viktor, 3
Frege, Gottlob, 36
Freud, Sigmund, 3
    engagement and challenge to
        Merleau-Ponty, 11
    reductionism, 15–16, 47–48
    Wittgenstein's sister a patient of, 36

Freudian psychoanalysis, 10, 43, 73
Frost, Robert, 73
Fusion of horizons, 25, 107, 112

G

Gadamer, Hans-Georg
    constructive resources for clinical
        work, 108–114
    fusion of horizons, 25
    hermeneutic humanism, 117–118
    hermeneutic practice as critique,
        105–107
    hermeneutics, 41
    life and work, 100–101
    and Merleau-Ponty, 68
    philosophical hermeneutics, 103–105
    reading, 101–103
    understanding and compassion,
        114–117
    vs Wittgenstein, 35
    works of:
        Gadamer in Conversation, 118
        Truth and Method, 11, 101
Gadamer: A Guide for the Perplexed
    (Lawn), 118
Gadamerian hermeneutics, 108
Gadamer in Conversation (Gadamer),
    118
Gallagher, Shaun, 61
Geisteswissenschaften (social sciences
        and humanities), 26, 103–104
Gendlin, Eugene, 3
Gesprächspartner (dialogue) , 28
Gestalt psychologists, 1, 73
Gestalt psychology, 10, 11, 56, 58, 123
Gestalt shift, 112
Gestalt therapists, 15, 24
Gestalt therapy, 10, 27, 40, 100, 106, 123
Gospel in Brief (Tolstoy), 37, 52
Grondin, Jean, 117
Guilt, 29, 86

H

Habermas, Jürgen, 33, 79, 101, 105
Healing through meeting, 27
Hegel, Georg W. F., 28, 32, 70
Heidegger, Martin
    concept of humanism, 6–7
    everyday worlds are primordial
        sources of meaning, 40

humanism and traditional
        metaphysics, 31
    humanists, 8
    influence on works of others, 12–13
    lecture on Aristotle, 9
    Levinas view of, 79–80
    mentor to Gadamer, 100
    vs Merleau-Ponty, 11
    and Wittgenstein, 35
    works of:
        Being and Time, 12, 59, 78, 88, 108
        "Letter on Humanism", 6, 7, 117
        Rektoratsrede, 88
Hermeneutic dialogue, 109
Hermeneutic humanism, 117–118
Hermeneutic practice as critique,
        105–107
Hermeneutics
    defined, 123
    dialogic, 108, 110, 116, 117
    dialogue, 109
    Gadamer, Hans-Georg, 41
    and humanistic tradition, 117
    intellectual and inspirational
        resource, 108
    philosophic, 11
    philosophical, 105, 106
    reductionism, 111
    search for meaning, 41
    study of meaning and interpretation,
        100–101, 103
    of suspicion, 114
    of trust, 107
    of understanding, 104, 118
Hermeneutic spirit, 14, 33, 56
Hermeneutic therapeutic sensibility, 14
Hermes, 103
Hertwig, Monika, 86
Hitlerism, 81, 84
Holism, 40, 58
Holistic phenomenology, 60
Holocaust memoir, 83–84, 86
Horizon, 6, 9, 59, 112, 123
Horizontverschmelzung (fusion of
        horizons), 25, 107, 112
Hospitality, 89–90
Human being (*Dasein*), 78, 108
Human condition, 29
Humanism. See also Humanistic
        psychotherapies
    believing, 16, 18, 31–33

ethical, 95–97
phenomenological, 35
question of, 6–9
Humanistic psychotherapies, 3, 5, 16, 62, 101, 117–118
Humanistic tradition, 8, 117
Human nature, 16
Human sexuality, 73–74
Hume, 67
Husserl, Edmund
and empathy, 87–88
father of phenomenological movement, 5
founder of phenomenology, 21
Gadamer read, 100
internal time-consciousness, 42
Levinas learned from, 78
Merleau-Ponty inspired by, 55
Merleau-Ponty studies manuscripts of, 58
and phenomenology, 59, 73

I

I and Thou, 10, 18–24, 105
I and Thou (Buber), 9, 17, 21, 34
Ich-Du, 18, 33, 108
Idealism, 123
I-It relations, 18, 19, 30, 33, 92
Implicit
accounts of human good, 108
and conversation, 107
defined, 123
and explicit dualisms, 72
and explicit forms of participation, 115
interpretive process, 116
Inauthenticity, 89, 90, 106
Inclusion (*Umfassung*)
about, 24–27
and confirmation, 27, 28
confirmation and, 28
contributions of Buber, 15, 16
defined, 123
dialogic, 51, 105
humanistic tradition, 8
irreducible proximity, 91
question of, 12–13
Individual experience, 75
Individual mind/brain, 61
Induction, 123

Inheritance (PBS), 86
In-itself and for-itself, 56
Inside-outside dualism, 58, 59, 69, 72
Inside-outside opposition, 60
Intellectualism, 56, 67
Intentionality, 87, 123
Interhuman, 24, 27, 33, 87, 91
Interlocutor
and conversation, 100, 108
in dialogue as partners, 104
and emotion, 69
fusion of horizons, 107
Gadamerian hermeneut, 118
gestalt shift, 51
listening hermeneut, 115
reduced to presence of object, 91
Wittgenstein's questions, 39, 46
Internal contradiction, 79
Internal dialogues, 38
Internal monologue, 23
Internal object, 40
Internal time-consciousness, 42
Internal truths, 113
Interpretation/gratification duality, 115
Interpretive expert-authority, 106
Interpretive process, 116
Intersubjective field, 3, 44, 67, 69
Intersubjective mutual regulation, 20
Intersubjective systems psychoanalysis, 16, 74
Intersubjective systems theory
and compassion, 114
defined, 123
embodied in relational contexts, 19
organizing principles, 111
primary intersubjectivity, 22
relational psychoanalysis, 3, 10, 19
self psychology and, 74
Intersubjectivity
in asymmetry of Levinasian ethics, 87
communion, 68
conceptions of, 22
defined, 75, 123
field theory of, 11
non-symmetrical relation, 88
and reversibility, 67–70
Intimacy of therapeutic encounter, 18
Intimate contact, 18
Intimate dialogic contact, 18
Intimate form of you, 18

Intrapsychic and relational, 72
Intricacy, 71, 124
Intuition, 24, 96, 124
Irigaray, Luce, 13
Irreducibility, 31, 71, 82, 93
Isolated-mind, 10, 68, 124
I-Thou encounter, 15
I-Thou relation, 91
I-You
    complete mutuality, 22
    concept of confirmation, 27
    genuine human dialogue, 31
    humanistic psychotherapists, 16
    inclusion opposite of empathy, 24
    intimate dialogic contact, 18
    is primal, 19, 32
    relatedness to natural world, 21
    spoken with whole being, 25, 26
    and We, 23
    word (*dabar*), 22

J

Jacobs, Lynne, 3, 19, 64
James, William, 12
Jewish mysticism, 21
Jewish studies, 17
Jonas, Helen, 86
Journal d'un Curé de Campagne [The
    Diary of a Country Priest]
    (Bernanos), 90
Judaism, 77
Jung, Carl G., 15, 16

K

Kafka, Franz, 71
Kant, Immanuel, 13, 16, 33, 37, 67
Kantian-inspired justice, 106
Kaufmann, Walter, 18
Kleinian, 3, 47
Knowing, 117
Knowledge
    abstracted, 63
    I-You, 31
    objectifying reductions, 82
    otherwise than being or, 80
    outside or abstracted, 63
    participation in Ideas, 26
    perceptual faith, 66
    scientific, 61

    self-becoming, 28
Kohut, Heinz, 1, 8, 74, 95, 114
Kohutian self psychology, 3, 30
Kristeva, Julia, 13

L

La durée (lived duration), 78
Lachmann, Frank, 64
Language
    communication, 22–23
    complexity of meanings, 41
    event experience vs accumulated
        learning, 102
    experience-distant, 57
    grammar, 40
    is essentially dialogic, 23
    patient, 103
    picture theory of, 38
    translation and philosophers, 102
    ways of talking, 47
    and world relations, 37
Language-game (*Sprachspiel*)
    attentiveness to difference, 51
    authoritarian approaches, 51–52
    causes, 48
    and compassion, 114
    concept of, 102
    cultures or forms of life, 41
    defined, 124
    of dissembling, 44
    encounter, 33
    key idea of Wittgenstein, 10
    meaning-as-use, 40–43
    objectifying language, 46
    and reality, 63–64
    say something unpredictable, 40
    of scientific justification, 50
    thought-experiment, 49
    words as pieces in, 39
Leading edge, 67
Lear, Jonathan, 21
Le chair (flesh), 74, 123
Les Temps Modernes (Sarte), 56
"Letter on Humanism" (Heidegger), 6,
    7, 117
Levinas, Emmanuel
    authenticity or sincerity, 88–90
    big idea of, 79–83
    and Buber, 90–92
    ethical humanism, 95–97

and human uniqueness, 32
influenced by Rosenzweig, 17
influences on, 77
intersubjective constitution of
    experience, 87
Levinasian therapeutics, 93–95
life and work, 78–79
moral status of animals, 8
subject after, 86–88
trauma and testimony, 83–86
and Wittgenstein, 35
Western philosophy, 77
works of:
    Ethics and Infinity, 97
    *Otherwise than Being, or Beyond
        Essence*, 79, 81, 83
    *Theory of Intuition in Husserl's
        Phenomenology*, 97
    Totality and Infinity, 79, 80, 82
    "Useless Suffering", 87
Levinas: An Introduction (Davis), 97
Levinasian humanism, 96–97
Levinasian therapeutics, 93–95
Library of Living Philosophers (Schilpp),
    17
Life, complicated form of, 41–42
Limited freedom, 66
Listening, 16, 43, 105, 115
Lived duration (*la durée*), 78
Loewald, 1
Logic, 35, 36
Logical content vs ethical thinking, 37
Logical positivism, 124
Loneliness and loss, 21
Looking, 43
Loss, 110
Losses of philosophers, 17
Ludwig Wittgenstein (Monk), 53

M

Mahler, Gustav, 16
*Martin Buber on Psychology and
        Psychotherapy* (Buber), 34
Maslow, Abraham, 8
Marx, 11, 107
Marxism, 56–57
Maslow, Abraham, 3
Master-slave dialectic, 70, 88
Material conditions, 61–62
Materialism, 124

May, Rollo, 3
Meaning-as-use, 10, 38, 39–40, 40–43,
    124
Memory, 29, 72–73, 78, 81, 83, 110
Mentalization theory, 48, 68
Merkwürdigkeit (oddness), 39
Merleau-Ponty (Carman), 76
Merleau-Ponty, Maurice
    clinical implications, 62–64
    cognitive neuroscience without
        reductionism, 60–62
    emotions and feelings, 47
    human life, 70–71
    intersubjectivity and reversibility,
        67–70
    learned from Husserl, 58
    and Levinas, 87
    life and work, 55–57
    perception and embodiment, 58–60
    possibly an atheist, 8
    and psychoanalysis, 73–75
    reading, 57
    skilled coping and situated
        temporality, 64–67
    traumatic living memory, 72–73
    vs Heidegger's being-in-the-world,
        59–60
    vs Wittgenstein, 35
    works of:
        Phenomenology of Perception, 10,
            56, 57, 59, 76
        Structure of Behavior, 56
        World of Perception, 76
Metaphysics, 31, 124
Methodical doubt, 58
"*Me voici*", 81, 83, 89
Mill, John Stuart, 3
Mind
    and body dualism, 44
    body-world, 74
    bond between soul and body, 62
    Cartesian, 44
    as container of ideas or pictures, 48
    emotions and feelings, 47
    isolated philosophy, 6, 68–69
    no-longer isolated, 55
    reified individual, 52
    representational theories of, 61, 64
    self-enclosed, 45
Mind-body dualism, 55, 58, 68, 69, 72,
    122

Mirror, reflection in, 69
Mirroring, 30
Mismeeting, 17, 19
Mitchell, Stephen, 1, 110
Moral phenomenology, 71
Moral status of animals, 8
Mutual recognition, 16, 19

N

Nagel, Thomas, 61
National Socialism, 79–80, 81
Natural attitude, 21
Natural sciences, 6, 103
Natural world, 21
Naturwissenschaften (natural sciences),
    6, 26, 103
Nazism, 78, 101
Neiman, Susan, 87
Neuropsychoanalysts, 6
Neuroscience, 31, 62. *See also* Cognitive
    neuroscience
Neurotic guilt feelings, 29
Nietzsche, 3, 16, 88
Nonneurotic guilt, 29
Non-symmetrical relation, 88
Nonverbal background, 14
Nussbaum, Martha, 13

O

Objective existence, 45
Object relations theory, 40, 45, 70–71
Observation, objects of, 31
Oddness (*Merkwürdigkeit*), 39
Ogden, Thomas, 64
Ontic, 26
Ontically, 26
Ontological, 26
Ontology, 79, 89, 91, 124
Ordinary-language philosophy, 35
Organizing principles, 5, 65, 75, 107, 111,
    124
Other (*Autrui*), 80, 81, 89, 90, 93, 108
Otherwise than Being, or Beyond Essence
    (Levinas), 79, 81, 83
Outside or abstracted knowledge, 63

P

Pain-language, 44
Participation (*Dabeisein*), 26

Participation in Ideas, 26
Partner, 10, 28, 104
Patient
    analysands, 114
    and clinician, 14
    embodied perception viewpoint, 62
    existential guilt, 29
    experience-near concepts, 94
    and experiential world, 65, 111, 115
    language, 103
    and loss, 110
    memories return, 50
    neurotic guilt feelings, 29
    objectifying labels, 50
    self-description, 111
    and skilled coping, 66–67
    and suicide attempt, 113
    working in the interhuman, 27
    work of inclusion, 26
Peirce, Charles Sanders, 12, 62
Perception, 57, 58, 59, 60, 73
Perceptual faith, 66, 124
Perspectival realism, 25
Phenomenologist, 10, 45, 47, 51
Phenomenology
    advent, 67
    and cognitive neuroscience
        dialogues, 62
    defined, 124
    empirical sciences and perception, 60
    of existence incarnate, 64
    existential, 74
    internal time-consciousness, 42
    lived experience, 78
    and Merleau-Ponty, 56, 58, 73
    natural attitude, 21
    and science, 61
    study of, 12
    Wittgenstein vs other philosophers,
        35
Phenomenology of Perception (Merleau-
    Ponty), 10, 56, 57, 59, 76
Philosophers
    atheist, 8
    comparison of, 11–12
    feminist, 13
    humanistic tradition, 8
    and natural sciences, 6
    traumatic losses and searching for
        sense, 17
    20th century European, 9, 10, 12, 35

understanding European, 103
  women, 13
Philosophical hermeneutics, 103–105,
  106
Philosophical Investigations
  (Wittgenstein), 10, 38, 39
Philosophical reflection, 37, 45
Philosophical therapy, 39
Philosophic hermeneutics, 11
Philosophy
  automaticity, 5–6
  body-in-the-world, 57
  conception of cure, 52
  of consciousness, 57
  critical, 67
  dialogic, 12, 109
  of embodiment, 59
  an ethical task, 36
  ethics is first, 79
  of infinite responsibility, 97
  of lived duration (*la durée*), 78
  organizing principles, 5
  understanding, 103
  working on oneself, 40
Phronesis (practical wisdom), 108, 117,
  118, 124
Physical sciences, 26
Picture-theory of ideas, 48
Picture theory of language, 38
Plato, 13, 26, 100, 109
Plurality, 3, 42
Poland, Warren, 95
Political blindspots of traumatic origins,
  82
Politics and ethics, 117
Popper, Karl, 47
Positive aggression, 82
Postmodernism, 12, 79, 112, 125
Post-traumatic stress disorder, 29
Practical wisdom. *See Phronesis*
  (practical wisdom)
Pragmatism, 12, 106, 125
Preconceptions, 43, 51, 58, 111
Primary intersubjectivity, 22
Principia Mathematica (Russell), 36
Private language, 43, 44, 45
Proprioception, 60, 69, 125
Proximity, 81, 91, 93, 114, 125
Psychoanalysis
  abstinence and nongratification of,
  90

clinical work of, 43
  clinical work vs theories, 3
  compassion, 116
  critical and constructive, 105
  descriptive phenomenology, 111
  Gadamerian hermeneutics, 108
  Gadamer's influence on, 101
  Gestalt therapy, 106
  great innovators in, 5
  meaning in theoretical discourse
    in, 40
  and Merleau-Ponty, 57, 73–75
  relational gestalt therapy, 10
  study of, 13
  therapeutic process, 48
  training in, 1
  traumatized self, 85
  understanding of, 2
Psychoanalytic phenomenologist, 94
Psychoanalytic tradition, 14, 94–95
Psychology, 48, 56

R

Ramsey, David, 37
Rationalism, 56, 67, 79, 125
Rawls, John, 33, 79
Reasons, 43, 47, 48
Reciprocity, 21, 92, 94
Recognition
  Anerkennung, 28
  confirmation, 29, 30
  emotional memory, 72
  and ethical relation, 92
  mutual, 16, 19
  skilled coping, 66
Reductionism
  biological/pharmacological, 1
  challenge by Merleau-Ponty, 56
  critique of objectifying reductions, 82
  defined, 125
  and Freud, 15–16
  genuine human dialogue, 31
  and hermeneutics, 111
  hermeneutic therapeutic sensibility,
    14
  humanistic tradition, 8
  and language-games, 42
  misses family resemblance, 50
  opposed by Wittgenstein, 47

resistance to scientific, 43
of scientific rationality, 10
Reductive gaze, 70
Reflection
    of Being on itself, 32
    dialogic, 94
    and lived relationship, 19
    in mirror, 69
    moral phenomenology, 71
    philosophical, 37, 45
    sedimentation, 65
Reification, 72, 125
Reified individual, 52
Rektoratsrede (Heidegger), 88
Relation, 19, 20, 21–22, 28, 30
Relational experience, 19
Relational gestalt therapists, 3
Relational gestalt therapy, 10
Relational matrix, 3
Relational psychoanalysis
    Buber unnoticed in psychoanalytic
        world, 15
    and compassion, 114
    and confirmation, 27
    defined, 125
    influential humanistic
        psychotherapies, 16
    intersubjective systems theory, 3,
        10, 19
    recognition, 30
    and systems view, 110–111
Religion
    Asian, 24
    and authenticity, 88
    and dialogic encounter, 33
    examination of religious texts, 32
    Freud dismissive of religious
        experience, 15
    glory of the Infinite, 85
    history of world, 12
    Jewish studies, 17
    Judaism, 77
    and Levinasian humanism, 96–97
    Levinas was a Talmudic scholar, 78
    Merleau-Ponty born Catholic and
        Cartesian, 56
    nondogmatic, 16
    pilgrims of Buber's religious works,
        21
    and Talmud, 79, 80
    theodicy, 87

worship of science, 47
Representationalism, 49, 60–61, 80, 125
Representationalist temptation, 48
Representational theories, 61, 64
Resoluteness, 88
Responsibility, 33
Reversibility, 67–70
Ricoeur, Paul, 8, 79, 107, 114
Rogers, Carl, 3, 15, 30
Rosenzweig, Franz, 17
*Routledge Philosophy Guidebook
    to Wittgenstein and the
    Philosophical Investigations*
    (McGinn), 53
Russell, Bertrand, 36, 37

S

Sartre, Jean-Paul, 7–8, 55–56, 56–57, 66,
    70, 77
Sass, Louis, 8
Saying vs Said, 83, 85, 89–90, 93
Schindler's List (Spielberg), 86
Schleiermacher, Friedrich, 14, 103
Schnitzler, Arthur, 16
Schopenhauer, 3, 52
Scientific justification, 50
Scientific rationality, 10
Search for meaning, 41
Search for truth, 108
Sedimentation, 65, 72, 110, 125
Seeing-as, 10, 125
Sein und Zeit. See Being and Time
    (Heidegger)
Self, 86–87
Self-becoming, 28
Self-being, 28, 86
Self-chosen life, 88
Self-description, 111
Self-development, 3
Self-identification, 93
Selfobject, 40, 125
Self psychology, 3, 8–9, 30, 40, 74, 114
Sensory process, 64
Shame, 46
Shoah, 85, 110, 125
Sincerity, 88, 89–90
Skepticism, 5, 125
Skilled coping, 64–67, 125
Sluga, Hans, 46, 50

Social sciences and humanities
(*Geisteswissenschaften*), 26,
103–104
Socrates, 2, 3, 35, 38, 71, 105
Solicitude, 23, 91
Solipsism, 10, 126
Speaking
aggressively, 69
basic word I-You, 26
communal, 22
forms of life, 46
of I-You relatedness, 21
and language, 23
personal making present, 2
a second language, 102
the unspeakable, 72, 84–85
Speciesism, 7, 31, 32, 126
Spielberg, Steven, 86
Sprachspiel. See Language-game
(*Sprachspiel*)
Staemmler, Frank-M., 3
Stern, Daniel, 20
Stern, Donnel, 64
Stoics, 8
Stolorow, Robert, 1, 13, 50, 61
Stone, Leo, 95
Structure of Behavior (Merleau-Ponty),
56
Structure of wholeness, 59
Subjection of Women (Mill), 3
Subjection to the other, 96
Subjectivism, 6–7
Subjectivity
body-subject, 69
epiphenomenon, 11
and ethical demands, 86
intertwined with others, 10
is life in the world, 46
and material conditions, 61–62
as objective existence, 45
and private-language argument, 44
skilled coping, 64
as subjection to the other, 96
Subject-object dualism, 58, 122
Substance, 35, 126
Substitution, 85, 93–94, 96, 126
Suffering person, 110
Suicide, 36, 113
Surprise, 18, 19, 20, 23, 112
Survivor of trauma, 77
Systems of communication, 40

Systems theory, 58

T
Tales of the Hasidim (Buber), 17
Talmud, 79, 80
Temporality, 67, 78, 91, 108, 109
Theodicy, 87
Theoretical knowing (*episteme*), 117
Theories of justice, 108
*Theory of Intuition in Husserl's
Phenomenology* (Levinas), 78
Theory of truth, 107
Therapeutic process, 48
Thinking
automaticity, 4
and dialogic, 7
distinguish from talking, 26
embodied, 65
forms of critique, 104–105
importance for clinicians, 3–4
logical content vs ethical, 37
persuasion over, 2
supports creativity, 5
Thought-experiment, 49
Thrownness, 126
Time and Free Will (Bergson), 78
Tolstoy, Leo, 52
Totality and Infinity (Levinas), 79, 80, 82
Tractatus Logico-Philosphicus
(Wittgenstein), 37, 38, 52
Trauma
clinical understanding of, 13
and devastation, 71
emotional memory, 72
Hitlerism, 81
losses of philosophers, 17
memories/understanding dissociated
by shock, 50
and perceptual faith, 66
and personal experience, 82
post-traumatic stress disorder, 29
relational experience, 19
skilled coping, 64, 65
survivor of, 77
and testimony, 83–86
and uncertainty, 21
Traumatic devastation, 21, 81, 82
Traumatic living, 72–73
Traumatic living memory, 83–85
Traumatic losses, 17

Traumatic relational experience, 19
Traumatic shock, 50
Traumatic suffering, 87
Traumatic testimony, 85–86
Traumatism, 85
Traumatized self, 85
Trüb, Hans, 16, 18, 26–27
Truth and Method (Gadamer), 11, 101
Twain, Mark, 102

U

Umfassung, 24, 26. *See also* Inclusion
    (*Umfassung*)
Uncertainty, 21
Unconscious, concept of, 3, 48–49, 74
Unconscious and conscious, 72, 74
Understanding
    about subject matter, 104
    and causes, 48
    and compassion, 114–117
    consciousness, 60
    and conversation, 11–12, 105
    dialogic, 99, 102, 104, 112
    and dialogic inclusion, 25
    dialogue, 12
    dissociated by traumatic shock, 50
    emergent in dialogue, 101, 107
    European philosophers, 103
    experiential world, 112
    of hermeneutics, 104, 118
    of human being (*Dasein*), 78
    individual mind/brain, 61
    is curative, 14
    philosophers, 4
    philosophy of, 103
    process of, 113
    psychoanalysis, 2
    search for truth and, 108
    and tradition, 109
    Verstehen, 26
    work of, 99–100
Unspeakable, 72, 73, 84, 85, 110
"Useless Suffering" (Levinas), 87

V

Vergegmung, 17, 126
Verständigung (coming-to-an-
    understanding), 118
Verstehen, 26

Visible and the Invisible (Merleau-
    Ponty), 57, 69, 75

W

Weininger, Otto, 36
Weltlichkeit, 7, 126
Western metaphysics, 31
Western philosophy, 1, 2, 7, 77
Whitehead, Alfred North, 36
Winkler, Paula, 16
Winnicott, Donald W., 3, 20, 95
Wittgenstein, Karl, 36
Wittgenstein, Leopoldine, 36
Wittgenstein, Ludwig
    contributions of, 16
    interest in, 12
    life and work, 36–38
    meaning as use in language-game,
        40–43
    reading, 38–40
    resources for clinicians, 43–50
    20th-century European philosopher,
        9
    a Wittgensteinian clinical sensibility,
        50–53
    works of:
        Philosophical Investigations, 10,
            38, 39
        Tractatus Logico-Philosphicus, 37,
            38, 52
Wittgenstein, Paul, 36
Wittgensteinian clinical sensibility,
    50–53
Wittgensteinian therapeutics, 43
Women philosophers, 13
Word (*dabar*), 22, 23–24, 44, 51, 71
Working models, 65
World of Perception (Merleau-Ponty), 76
World relations, 37

Z

Zahavi, Dan, 47, 88
Zionism, 17
Zulu single sentence-word, 19
Zweig, Stefan, 16